Silver
LININGS IN DARK CLOUDS

Copyright ©2022 Silverline Dennis Dic-Fiberesima.
All rights reserved. First paperback edition printed 2022
in the United Kingdom.
ISBN 978-1-913455-54-5
No part of this book shall be reproduced or transmitted in
any form or by any means, electronic or mechanical, including
photocopying, recording, or by any information retrieval system without
prior written permission of the publisher.
Published by Scribblecity Publications.
Printed in Great Britain.
Although every precaution has been taken in the preparation of this
book, the publisher and author assume no responsibility for errors or
omissions. Neither is any liability assumed for damages resulting from
the use of this information contained herein.

Silverline Dennis Dic-Fiberesima
1936- 2022

DEDICATION

This book is dedicated to God Almighty, the Pilot of my ship of life when the current was drifting, the tempest blistering, the wind bulldozing, and the enemies secretly attacking and threatening. The effects of all those circumstances made me faint, but He sustained me, brought me and all that is mine to safety. To my generation, as a legacy to pass on to my children and their generations, a baton of faith for them to walk in the light of the Lord's Word.

ACKNOWLEDGEMENTS

I acknowledge the amiable contributions of my daughter, Dakoru, who put pressure on me to put my life's experiences in writing to help others avoid my mistakes and emulate the virtues God deposited in me. She bore the cost of editing the book and made sure it was registered and published. The book could not have seen the light of day without her tireless efforts. I owe her my gratitude. May the Lord Jesus supply all her needs. Amen. I won't fail to mention Timi Yeseibo, the Editor who did a meticulous work in editing the book.

TABLE OF CONTENTS

Foreword		vii
Chapter 1:	Silver Linings in Dark Clouds	9
Chapter 2:	Going to School	22
Chapter 3:	My First Work Experience	34
Chapter 4:	Marriage to Hon. Dennis Dic-Fiberesima	41
Chapter 5:	A Quiver Full of Arrows	54
Chapter 6:	The Okrika Crisis	64
Chapter 7:	the Biafran War	71
Chapter 8:	Life After the War	87
Chapter 9:	My Husband's Deliverance	98
Chapter 10:	My Retirement From Teaching	111
Chapter 11:	Legacy	122

FOREWORD

Life is a mystery bag of light that shines out of the thickest darkness. Every dark cloud has its peculiar silver lining. Therefore, weeping may endure for the night, but joy comes in the morning. *Silver Linings in Dark Clouds* by Silverline Dennis Dic-Fiberesima is the autobiography of my aunty, the only sister of my late father, Elder S. D. J. Ogan. It is the story of a life full of grace and glory amid trials and tribulations. It is the exciting account of the vision and vicissitudes of a mother and grandmother, from the time of going to school, first work experience, and marriage to Hon. Dic-Fiberesima, Dennis. It also tells the story of her 'Quiver full of Arrows', the Crisis in Okrika, the Nigerian Civil War, various deliverances in the family, retirement, and her legacy.

Mummy Silverline's life journey is indeed the story of 'Silver Linings in Dark Clouds'. It is an account of triumphs amid tribulations, a fantastic story of what God can do with a life fully dedicated and yielded to Him. This book is an indispensable reading for all, particularly the children, grandchildren, and great-grandchildren. It is instructive to all those who see dark clouds without the silver linings around them. I heartily recommend it to all and sundry.

Dr Steve Ogan
Port Harcourt, Nigeria

Chapter 1

SILVER LININGS IN DARK CLOUDS

ı mua nyo ı mo nemika bebe, ı bo nyo won nemi.
If you are not sure where you are going, at least be sure of where you are coming from. - Okrika Proverb

Four months after I was born, my mother was arrested and sent to prison. During the nine months that she was away, my father had to step into his new role, and became my mother. When I would cry, my father would pick me up and cradle me close to his chest, where my ravenous mouth would automatically reach for his breast. Only after I sucked his empty breast would my ceaseless crying stop, and I would gradually fall asleep.

In those days, infant formula or bottle-feeding was non-existent in my community. We lacked nurses to offer guidance on infant care. My mother had a healthy pregnancy, and a local midwife attended to her delivery at home because there was no hospital or clinic in our town. My grandparents had already passed, and there was no close relative to assist my father. He was left helpless with the harrowing task of caring for an infant. My endless crying touched sympathizers who came to help my father care for me, and they too were sometimes moved to tears and would cry along with me.

My father became resourceful and would feed me flakes of fresh fish, which he had carefully deboned, salted, steamed and mashed. He would put the fish into my eager hungry mouth, a little at a time. He would also give me *adu*, which is part of the family of the three-leaved cluster yam, but a smaller variety. After cooking and removing the skin, he would crush the *adu* to a pulp and feed me; giving me sips of water if I was thirsty.

In this way, God's eyes watched over me like He watches over little sparrows, and He kept me alive in His mercy until my mother returned.

My mother's name was Eunice Jones Tamuno-Orunengime Ogan, and my My father's mother, Madam Dukoseipirima Tamuno-Orunengime Ogan had brought my mother to Okrika from Ibo land, which is in eastern Nigeria, when she was young. In those days, chiefs from the riverine areas and coastal towns that border the Atlantic Ocean in the southern part of Nigeria served as middlemen in the slave trade. They bought slaves from the hinterland. They also brought people to increase the number of their families and bolster their war canoes. I don't know the circumstances surrounding my mother's arrival in the Ogan household, but she lived with my grandmother until she grew to womanhood. Then she was betrothed to my father. We had no records of her birth or lineage.

Being a diligent worker, my mother used to buy small dried fish and crayfish which she sold at Elelenwo market. Her customers who hailed from Igboland nicknamed her *Nwanyi Ocha*, which means white woman, because she was very fair in complexion and beautiful. Nwanyi Ocha eventually became the name that she was called in our neighbourhood.

Despite her lack of formal education, she figured out how to brew gin which tasted like brandy by cleverly blending palm wine with sugar. In a covered drum with a pipe attached, she would then heat the mixture, and the liquid-form of the condensed vapour will pass through the pipe into another container. This is chemistry. Till date, we still don't know how she acquired the knowledge.

In those days, the British colonial authorities were in charge, although they also administered government through the local chiefs using a system of indirect rule. Nigerians' first contact with Europeans was with the Portuguese, with whom they traded in spices, spirits, firearms, and other goods, including slaves, in the fifteenth century. The British arrived in the sixteenth century and by the eighteenth century, they had overtaken the Portuguese in slave trade.

British colonial rule in Nigeria began as an attempt to end slave trade and establish legitimate commerce in other goods, like palm produce. The Abolition Act of 1807 was passed by the British Parliament, declaring slave trade illegal. Using treaties and military might including their gunboats, Britain gained control of the coastal regions in the south and the hinterlands, extending to the northern part of the country. In 1914, the two British colonies in the southern and northern parts of the country of what is now Nigeria were merged to become the Colony and Protectorate of Nigeria.

Imported liquor served as currency and a revenue earner for the authorities. Slaves were traded in exchange for liquor, and even after slave trade was abolished; gin currency was still prevalent in the palm produce trade. Custom duties on liquor made up half of the annual revenue from southern Nigeria, and World War I resulted in the gradual decline in the use of gin currency and a steady transition to a monetized economy.

British companies sold Stock gin, whisky, wine, brandy, and so on, at expensive prices accessible only to chiefs and the wealthy. They however observed that the indigenous people drank locally brewed gin called hot, which was cheap. To avoid competition and maintain revenues from liquor importation, the colonial authorities declared brewing gin illegal.

Christian missionaries were already in Nigeria at that time, and they had established missions and churches. One may wonder if they had a problem with their converts drinking alcohol. Trade in liquor incited fierce debates, and the Church Mission Society was among the groups opposed to it. However, the reality was that the church in our hometown did not have an issue with people drinking local gin. Even the pastors drank gin. There were no health officers or nutritionists to enlighten people on its effect on the body. All they knew was that it drove away cold, stimulated appetite, eased pain, and relaxed their bodies.

My mother's locally brewed gin sold like hot cake around Okrika and its environs to the envy of her competitors. They were so jealous that they conspired against her a few months after my birth. They accused her of brewing illicit gin and reported her to the authorities. Their actions remind me of an extract from a *Snow White* play in which I recited the following lines.

Oh! Jealousy, how pitiless,
The punishment thou art devices,
From out of the heart where thou dost dwell,
No gentle mercy ere arises.

The colonial authorities arrested her and sent her to Degema prison.

Early in the nineteenth century, the regions of Nigeria

that came under British control were grouped into protectorates, namely, Lagos, Niger Coast, also known as Oil Rivers, and Northern Protectorate. Lagos and Niger Coast Protectorate were merged in 1906 to become the Southern Protectorate, which initially had Western, Central, and Eastern provinces. Degema, which was part of the Eastern Province and a district headquarters for Okrika, was where my mother served her prison term.

In the Bible, the prophet Isaiah, writing about God's care for the chosen nation of Israel, asked rhetorically, "Can a woman forget her sucking child, that she should not have compassion on the son of her womb?" Then He answered, "Yea, they may forget, yet will I [God] not forget thee." (Isaiah 49:15)

My mother did not forget about me. While in custody, she slept on a cold floor crying for her baby as her breast milk flowed unabated. Her ordeal is better imagined than expressed. As I said earlier, God watched over me and kept me alive in His mercy until she returned.

***

I was born on 31 July 1936 in Ogan Ama, a township in Okrika Town. Okrika is situated in the Niger Delta region of southern Nigeria, and it is one of the nine ancient towns of the Okrika Kingdom and its capital. Other towns are Ogu, Bolo, Ogoloma, Ibaka Ogbogbo, Abuloma, Ele, and Isaka. Okrika is a port town and headquarters of Okrika local government area in present day Rivers State. It lies south of the state capital, Port Harcourt..

My late great-great-grandfather, Ilalamoku Ogan, founded Ogan Ama during the rule of King Fibika of Okrika Kingdom, and was first to settle at Ambeme biri (Ambeme quarters) in Okrika. He was very rich because he traded with the British who dominated trade in the region around the seventeenth century, and he later became a council chief and prominent man in the Ado royal family. The Ado royal family consists of the Ibanichuka, Fibika, Ogan, Dokube, and Abam families. The king or Amayanabo and his chiefs permitted him to live on his own because Ambeme biri became too small for him and his subjects. He then got a place at Tomo biri in Okrika, which is still called Ogan polo (Ogan community) today. After a while, they needed more space, so his subjects founded an island opposite Okrika town and named it Ogan, after him. It is now known as Ogan Ama.

Ogan Ama is one of the war canoe houses of the Ado royal house of Okrika. In those days, Communities in the Niger Delta then organized themselves into canoe houses, which were essentially trade and military cooperatives. Chiefs were required to own war canoes that could carry at least forty men who were prepared to protect trading routes and defend the community from enemy attacks. These men became part of a canoe house by either lineage or acquisition as slaves, and the chiefs took care of their upkeep.

Chief Ilalamoku Ogan's land was shared into seventeen compounds among his subjects. Fourteen compounds are in Ogan Ama, while three are still at Ogan polo. The compound heads are known as chiefs. The names of the compounds in Ogan Ama are given below.

1. Chief Atubona Chefonari Ilalamoku Ogan
2. Chief Amos Ilalamoku Ogan
3. Chief Edward Dalakabo Ilalamoku Ogan
4. Chief Samuel Ilalamoku Ogan
5. Chief Joseph Ilalamoku Ogan
6. Chief Tamuno Ilalamoku Ogan
7. Chief John Aberemangimari Ilalamoku Ogan
8. Chief Tamuno-Orunengime Ilalamoku Ogan
9. Chief Tamunobesiki Ilalamoku Ogan
10. Chief Uwakwe Ilalamoku Ogan
11. Chief Jonny Ibarakubieye Ilalamoku Ogan
12. Chief Panga Ilalamoku Ogan
13. Chief Joel Ilalamoku Ogan
14. Chief Moses Ilalamoku Ogan

The names of the compounds at Ogan polo are given below.

15. Chief Stephen Nwabianko Ilalamoku Ogan
16. Chief Solomon Nwanem Ilalamoku Ogan
17. Special compound of Chief Ilalamoku Ogan

My father was born into the family of Chief Tamuno-Orunengime and Madam Dukoseipirima Tamuno-Orunengime Ogan. He was the head of the Tamuno-Orunengime family, and he kept in a notebook the dates of birth of the children born in the compound. His parents were blessed with four biological children namely, Madam Ada Amos born in 1889; Madam Ngeribomieyeoforie Tamuno-Orunengime, born in 1892, died February 1950; their first son, Elder Augustus Tamuno-Orunengime Ogan, born in 1885, died in 1945; and my father, Elder Jones Tamuno-Orunengime Ogan, who was born in 1900 and died 6 October 1973. They were all born in Ogan Ama.

His father was a very rich palm oil trader, who traded with the British. He procured two slaves, Solomon Irebulam and his younger brother, Thomas, from Iboland. My father's education ended in standard five or primary five, because in those days education was not encouraged, and people were forced to go to school because they did not realize the value of education.

My father's family were members of the Anglican Communion. The earliest Christian missionary activity in Nigeria took place around the fifteenth century and was short-lived. Some factors responsible for this were the profitable slave trade and death of missionaries occasioned by malaria. The abolition of slave trade in the nineteenth century played a role in sparking interest in the redemption of Nigeria once again.

Between the mid to late 1800s, several Christian missions had an established presence in southern Nigeria, including the Wesleyan Methodist, Church Mission Society (CMS), United Presbyterian Church from Scotland, Southern American Baptist, and Qua Iboe Mission from protestant Ireland. At this time, freed slaves of Nigerian descent who had been settled in Sierra Leone returned to Nigeria and helped to evangelize the people.

Anglicanism flourished under Samuel Ajayi Crowther of the CMS. In 1866, King William Dappa Pepple of Bonny Island and his people were instrumental in Crowther establishing St. Stephens Church in Bonny, an Island in a coastal city in the Niger Delta which borders the Atlantic Ocean. By 1880, Anglicanism had spread to Okrika.

My father was a lay reader and preacher in our local church, St. Agnes Church, Ogan Ama. His dedication led to him being elected treasurer in 1940. He was so trustworthy and faithful that even when he pleaded to be relieved of this duty, all members of the church refused. He was treasurer of the church for thirty-three years, an honour that was recognized and appreciated until he passed.

He started a strong evangelical band in Okrika, which Elder Aaron Ogan, Elder George of George Ama, Elder Oluka of St. Martins Church; Ogu, and Madam Salome Aleli of St. James Church; Ogoloma, joined. They were dedicated to winning of souls. To the glory of God, the seed they sowed has today spread like wildfire to the Anglican Church in Okrika and beyond.

My parents had three boys before me; however, the second child died early on. I grew up as the last child and only daughter, and I was very close to my mother. In addition to the dried fish and crayfish that she sold at Elelenwo market, she sold some provisions like rice, onions, tin tomatoes, corned beef, salt, dried pepper, and snuff, at home. I helped her sell goods in her provision store, and I ran errands like collecting money from those who bought goods on credit.

She had total control of running the home, and my father who was a fisherman provided money for food and upkeep. He brought fishes home from his catches. I didn't eat a lot. Most times, after only licking the soup and eating the fish in the soup, I would feel full. Often, as my father ate, I would go close to him and ask for his fish, and he would always oblige.

Back then, we had neither electricity nor pipe-borne water, and at night when we fetched water from a well, we used bush lamps. Sometimes, if there was a big event like a wakekeep, they used a Tilley lamp, which produced a brighter light. My elder brothers would fetch water from the well and split firewood for cooking while I would wash the dishes, sweep our kitchen, and the areas outside our home. Since there were no blenders, when cooking, I would help my mother pound things in the mortar.

My father's age group in Ogan Ama was a unifying factor in the community, economically and socially, and they would organize social activities like wrestling and dancing. He was a good wrestler and was in the dancing group. All the members of his age group were fishermen, and they encouraged each other to build zinc houses by contributing money which they loaned to one another in turns. That was how my father built our house.

He used moulded, mud blocks for the walls and plastered them with a mixture of cement and sand. Our house had four rooms and a commodious parlour. The kitchen was separate from the house, like an outhouse, creating a kind of corridor between them. It had mud walls and a thatch roof as thatch was the common material for roofing in those days.

I grew up in a nuclear family with only my father, mother, and two elder brothers, and my family had just enough for our needs. My parents were honest and transparent. They were content with what they had. They did not borrow and never bought things on credit. Many relations brought precious things to my parents for safekeeping because they were trustworthy. Whenever the owners requested the items, my parents would give the items back to them. They were at peace with people. I believe that the love and trust one experiences in a nuclear family is deeper than that of an extended family, and I always felt loved by my parents and brothers. This was their legacy to me, and I believe it is worth emulating.

My full names are Silverline Ajinboyeseangake. There was no special naming ceremony for me. Ajinboyeseangake means I live with only what I have and not another's. Silverline means the light amid the cloud. In those days, parents or close elders simply named children according to their feelings or expectations. Perhaps those who named me could foresee that when ominous clouds gathered over my life, the light of God's divine presence would prevail.

Chapter 2

GOING TO SCHOOL

I am still learning. -Michelangelo

I started school early before what was considered school age because there was nobody to take care of me at home. I must have been four. My father was a fisherman, and my mother was a market trader. My brothers went to school, so I had to follow my immediate elder brother to his school. He took me to the ABC class as it was called then and advised me to be quiet, and listen to the teacher.

During my early years, there were only mission schools in my community. Missionaries established the first schools in Nigeria within their church premises which were funded and staffed by their agencies. Methodist Mission established the first primary school in the early 1840s in Badagry, Lagos. Missionaries saw education as a chief means of spreading Christianity and literacy, this was a means of enabling converts read the Bible for themselves. Beyond that, they also taught brickmaking, blacksmithing, carpentry, masonry, dressmaking, and domestic science. They trained their converts to be teachers, catechists, and clergymen, so they could be gainfully employed and better citizens.

The first school I attended was situated in my local church, St Agnes, Ogan Ama. Infant classes were held in the church building, and after church services on Sundays, the long benches were moved towards the altar, so that the open space created could be used for classes. It was a preparatory school to qualify pupils for primary school. I was attentive, so I learned quickly, and not too long after, I became the teacher's favourite. In the shortest time, I qualified to start primary one in 1944. At the age of eight, I started attending Okrika Boys' School.

Okrika Boys' School was located at Okrika town and had classes from standard one to six or primary one to six. It was a day school built within St. Peter's Church compound. It was a mixed school. There were no girls' school in Okrika probably because in those days, many people believed that educating girls was a waste of money: girls were only to be groomed for marriage, so only a few girls attended the school.

It was a model school which aimed to mould the character of pupils so they could become exemplary citizens. Parents co-operated wonderfully with the school, and if If their children misbehaved at home or refused to attend classes, they reported the matter to the headmaster. The headmaster would then send strong boys to bring the children to school, and he would discipline them. Teachers were highly respected in the community.

To attend school at Okrika town, school children from Ogan Ama had to cross the river by boat because there was no road connecting both islands. At ebb tide, adults could cross from Ogan Ama to Okrika on foot using the Ambeme biri axis. Ogan Ama to Ambeme biri by boat was about a hundred metres. However, at full tide, they paddled a canoe across. This was a daily routine, so people weren't afraid.

During one such crossing from Ogan Ama to Okrika to attend school in 1944, I was involved in a boat mishap. The tide was full, and the boat I was in capsized mid-river. I did not know how to swim. I was going down in the water, and all I heard was my elder brother's distress cry, 'Oh God! My sister!' Instantly, God in His compassion released His supernatural power and made me float. My brother swam and pushed me along until several canoes came to rescue the school children involved in the accident. One of the canoes picked me up and took me to safety.

Later in life, I came to understand that in accordance with His word in Isaiah 43:2, God had delivered me and preserved my life.

When thou passest through the waters, I will be with thee; and through the rivers, they shall not overflow thee.

In those days, mission schools' curriculum focused heavily on reading, writing, and arithmetic, and our timetable at Okrika Boys' School also featured subjects like geography.. Mr Bennet Kalio was my teacher in primary one. He was tall, huge, stately, and knowledgeable. His class was always lively, and he taught us inspiring songs that aroused our interest in learning. I share two of the songs below:

We are going to our classes with clean hands and faces
to pay great attention to what we are told
for learning is better than silver and gold,
for learning, is better, is better than silver and gold.

Little by little, says a taught boy,
moment by moment I will implore
learning a little every day,
And not wasting all my time in play,
The world would be a better place for me.

Mr Kalio gave me a solid foundation at the beginning of my primary education. After school, I did not waste time playing, and even while I helped in my mother's provision store, I studied my notes and memorized multiplication tables whenever there were no customers. Okrika and, indeed, Kalio Ama lost a genius at the news of his sudden death.. May his soul rest in perfect peace. Amen.

Primary six pupils were split into three classes which were handled by Mr Anya George, Mr Banigo

George, and Mr Godwin. I was in Mr Anya George's class. He was elderly, and he always dressed in three-quarter knickers and long stockings. He wore thick eyeglasses and kept a long cane on the teacher's table. The recommended textbooks for arithmetic were *Common Sense Arithmetic and Pendubry,* and during arithmetic class, he would set sums on the board from the textbook and ask us to solve them, and whenever we had difficulty solving the problems, and made noise to that effect, he would hit the table with the cane to inspire calmness. He would then remove his glasses, lift the textbook, and ask, 'Class, what is this?'

We would answer, 'Common Sense Arithmetic book.'

'Then, use your common sense!'

We would then encourage one another to use common sense. It was an interesting joke to us.

Our second teacher, Mr Banigo George, was young and handsome and was active in the social, religious, and political activities in George Ama. Our third teacher, Mr Godwin, taught us geography. Even though we were in primary school, we could vividly describe features of an island, lake, oasis, archipelago, estuary, tributary, ocean, sea, tableland, and so on. Our teachers were good and dedicated, and they taught above primary school level. My best subjects were arithmetic and geography.

***

Pupils were divided into five houses for inter-house sports competition. I was in Oputibeya House and competed in the 100m and 200m races, hurdles, calculation race, needle and thread race, bottle race, and sack race. For the calculation race, sums would be set on a board and participants were required to run to the board, solve the sums, and run back. I always won the calculation and the needle and thread races for my house.

Belicent Alabaraba, Bernice Oruene, and Gladys Imabibo were my friends in school. At home, we ate breakfast before we went to school. Our parents never gave us money to buy food during break period. They only gave us money for our transport. Belicent lived close to school. She normally went home to eat during break, and she would urge me to follow her home. Her mother hailed from Nembe, another ancient kingdom of the Niger Delta, and she had a calm temperament while her father usually went fishing at night. So by the time we got to her house, her mother would have prepared roasted fresh fish for us. We ate the fish and drank garri. Bernice Oruene was more mature than my other friends were. She was disciplined and caring. Gladys Imabibo was short, and she had a quiet disposition. My friends saw me as brilliant and unassuming.

I finished primary six in 1949. In Okrika Kingdom,

only Okrika Boys' School was qualified to conduct the School Leaving Certificate examination. I wrote the exams and made a distinction. The girls who performed well were given letters for an aptitude test and interview at Archdeacon Crowther Memorial Girls School (ACMGS), Elelenwo, while the boys were to be tested and interviewed at Okrika Grammar School in Okrika. Successful candidates were admitted into secondary schools.

Before my test and interview, I developed a big sore on the left side of my right knee. As I had no scratches before, I do not know what caused the sore. The painful sore took about three months to heal, and in that time, I had missed the test and interview, and lost a wonderful opportunity to attend the only girl's secondary school at the time.

My father took me to the general manager of schools, late Mr Efeture, and explained my plight. Mr Efeture forwarded a letter to the principal of ACMGS, who in her reply affirmed that admission had closed, and she could not oblige his request. While the prospects for my future was yet undetermined, the archdeacon of St. Peter's Church, Okrika, late Bishop Barahart, visited our church and my father, during their discussion, introduced me to him. He told my father that an unmarried female teacher had been dismissed for getting pregnant, and it was a golden opportunity for me to replace her. I grabbed the opportunity to teach at my former school without complaint. At that time, it was not uncommon that graduates of each level of education could become teachers of that level. So a graduate of primary school could teach primary school pupils.

My headmaster, late Mr Kemmer, was delighted to have me as a member of his staff. We had our teacher's quarters in the church compound. The other female teachers were more mature than I was. I gave them their due respect, and I was accepted, and was able to fit in with them.

Instead of Mr Kemmer to assign me to standard one or two, he led me to the standard three and introduced me as their new teacher. He did this because he knew I was intelligent, and he had confidence in my abilities. However, the mature boys in the class felt slighted that a feeble, little girl was their teacher.

They spoke to themselves in Okrika dialect, *'Iyo, ini wa dikisima okwu diki, ma kalatoku so bo ye se wadie, wa 'ma' se achin eke; miss ani wa se achin bia ye.'* This means, 'Boys, see how they have insulted us by bringing this little girl to teach us. We would not call her Ma, but we would call her Miss.'

I kept mute as if I did not hear what they said because they were ready to beat me up. They then decided to test my ability to teach. They brought tough questions on L.C.M., decimals, multiplication and division of fractions, inverse proportion, compound interest, and so on, from *Common Sense Arithmetic Book and Pendubry*, which covered standard six syllabus, for me to solve. Unknown to them, arithmetic was my best subject. I would state the problems step-by-step and teach them how to arrive at the answers. They were so confounded, they never underrated me again. That was how I gained their respect and confidence. I taught that class until I left for the Women Training College (WTC), Enugu, in January 1952.

Reflecting on that period, I see that God uses our disappointments to turn things around for our good. We should learn to give Him thanks for everything.

***

WTC Enugu was the first women's training centre in the then Eastern Region of Nigeria. It was set up to train teachers intending to teach in primary schools and as a home economics centre.

Initially, local mission schoolteachers were not trained or qualified because teacher training centres did not exist. For example, after completing primary school, I was appointed a teacher with no formal training. CMS founded the first teacher training institute around 1859 in Abeokuta, in western Nigeria. Shortly after, other missions did the same, and their aim was to produce classroom teachers, catechists, deacons, and priests.

Formal western education was solely a missionary effort until the colonial government began to participate through grants-in-aid and ordinances, but these early efforts did not make much impact. Following criticisms of the mission schools for their irrelevant curriculum (among others) by the Phelps Stokes Commission Report of 1922, the colonial administration instituted some reforms in teacher training.

Two types of teacher training institution were created, namely, the Elementary Training Centre (ETC), to provide a two-year course, leading to Teachers Grade III Certificate for lower primary school teachers and the Higher Elementary Training College (HETC), to provide a four-year course, leading to Teachers Grade II Certificate for senior primary teachers. My course at WTC, Enugu, fell into the latter category.

The principal and some of the staff of the college were European. Students from Okrika and environs travelled by train from Port Harcourt to Enugu, which was about 240 km away. The school arranged a special coach in the train for us, and the school van was always at the railway station awaiting our arrival. It was a boarding school, and they took good care of us. Sometimes, the principal would go to the kitchen and taste the food to ensure it was alright.

I had a friend called Diamond, and her father was European, while her mother came from Enugu area. She resembled her father. We were so close that our teachers acknowledged us as Silver and Diamond. During short breaks, I did not travel home, I stayed with one of our village elders, Elder Ezekiel Uwakwe Ogan, aka Papa Ukwu, who lived and worked in Enugu with his family. His son, George Ezekiel Ogan, came to cheer me up on visiting days. He was my only regular visitor.

Enugu was a regional capital and a coal city. Coal was discovered in 1909 at Udi Ridge, and this made the city a commercial hub, attracting miners and other migrants both locals and foreigners. The first consignment of coal was shipped from the new port at Port Harcourt to the United Kingdom in 1916. The Eastern Line railway was built to transport coal from Enugu to Port Harcourt. The railways and electric power companies were major domestic consumers of coal before the discovery of crude oil and subsequent decline of coal production.

Working conditions in the coalmines were poor. Coal workers were not provided with quality tools, and many of them lacked boots. They worked in close confinement in an atmosphere low on oxygen, hence the protest. The workers organized themselves into a union and agitated for better employment and working conditions. The refusal by the British companies to give in fully to their demands led to a sit-in at the mines and ultimately the government's use of force. In what is known as the Iva Valley Massacre, where twenty-one coal miners were killed while about fifty were injured in 1949. This incident was the catalyst for a united call for independence from British rule nationwide.

When we visited some of the historic coal mining

sites, we passed through tunnels that were cold and had water dripping from the top onto our heads. They were dark with poor lighting. The passages were small and looked like death traps. I'm convinced that the miners survived such conditions only by the mercy of God.

After two years' study at WTC, student teachers were sent to the field to teach junior primary pupils before they returned to complete their course. I was posted to St. Martins School, Ogu, where I taught from January 1954 to December 1955. In January 1956, I returned to complete my course. At the end of the training, successful students graduated as Grade two teachers, qualified to teach senior primary pupils. I graduated in 1957, having made five credits in one sitting.

Chapter 3

MY FIRST WORK EXPERIENCE

When you learn, teach. When you get, give. - Maya Angelou

I guess I should discount my experience teaching standard three pupils at Okrika Boys' School. In that case, my first work experience came after a couple of years training at WTC, Enugu, when I was posted to St. Martin's School, Ogu, in 1954, to teach infant classes only. The school was mixed, and it had classes for primary school. Ogu is one of the towns that make up the Okrika Kingdom. It is now part of the Ogu/Bolo local government area of Rivers State. The teachers' quarters were in the school compound.

While there, I exhibited the knowledge I had acquired. The primary school pupils would leave their classes to watch my pupils and me especially during physical training exercises. The school timetable always had

Physical Education (P.E.) in the morning, which was meant to exercise the body and stimulate the brain, and because of the training I had received, I taught every lesson using teaching aids. This made learning exciting for my students. However, this was not the case in the primary classes. The primary school pupils would beg me privately to teach them because they were terribly bored.

I was part of the school's drama group. I played the part of Snow White in one of the drama series. Being the only female teacher in the school, I played netball with the primary school girls who were mature, and we would have netball competitions with neighbouring schools and we would play well. My time at St. Martin's was impressive.

***

The social scene in Okrika at the time was taken with highlife music. Rex Lawson, who hailed from Kalabari tribe of the Niger Delta, made highlife popular in the south. His songs depicted the political uprising of the period.

> *Obona bere bote*
> *Obona bere bo te*
> *Buo bara fin ate*
> *Bere bo te*
> *Obona bere bo te*

This means, come and hear; problem has come. Leg has tied the hand. Problem has come. Come and hear; problem has come.

Ngowuka, from Bolo in Okrika kingdom, produced philosophical music, which was also in vogue. She and her team used clappers, native pot, and drums to produce sounds which inspired different dance steps. Many people invited her to grace their functions, and whenever I heard her music, I would start to shake my waist intuitively.

Tamuno bara atereaye bime
Tatariye ani dumo
Imain karamaye toku
Tere karamaye ani igbigi
Dumo oforika okuma yego fasam
Toku oforiko okuma igbela biabo oforiye
Igbigi oforika okuma Inigbela bia ochenemi
Tereaye ma aringba anwobime

This means, I ask these three things from God, first is life, second is child, third is money. If there is no life, everything is lost. If there is no child, nobody asks about you. If there is no money, the question is, what does he know? All the three, I need them.

Although people had adopted the dressing customs of the British, women never wore trousers in my hometown then. Men wore trousers and trouser suits.

In Okrika, traditional attires were worn to suit the occasion, and status was important and was reflected in the fashion of the times. For example, male elders dressed in tops that were called jumpers. Jumpers were made from five yards of fabric. They paired jumpers with trousers or they tied one fathom of *njiri* from their waist to ankles. A fathom is cut out from a roll of cloth, and it measures five and a half feet in length.

Chiefs wore top hats and don, and they used walking sticks. A don is a long shirt with a band collar that goes all the way to the ankles and usually worn over trousers. Kings adorned their heads with beautiful crowns and wore dons made from *feni* cloth known as *namatibi*, flag, *chirifiema*, and other high-quality fabrics. Their dons were made from eight yards of cloth and studded with gold, silver, or coral. They also carried a matching walking stick.

Women plaited their hair and wore gowns and skirt and blouse. They tied 'up and down' wrapper made from designs such as *feni, popo, ikaki ikpo, njiri, india, onungwa, ikpo* velvet, and so on, to suit the occasion and show their social status.

The 1950s saw an upsurge in the cry for independence from colonial rule. Political parties were formed and a constitutional conference was held. Crude oil was discovered in commercial quantities. Despite all these changes, society was still patriarchal: men were given the upper hand in the family and political structures. Career choices for women were limited, and the job opportunities available were teaching, nursing, midwifery, cleaning, and so on. In general, missionary education was geared towards making women good wives and home keepers rather than income earners.

As I said, many viewed educating females as a waste of time and money because they were bound to be wives, mothers, and keepers of the home. In retrospect, I see that my uneducated mother laid the foundation for my desire to go to school. I remember that when my parents received letters, they had to rely on others who were literate to read them. My mother often expressed her desire that I would not suffer a similar fate.

My eldest brother was a source of inspiration to me. He was intelligent, after he finished primary school, he qualified to attend Okrika Grammar School. Unfortunately, he had no sponsors and resorted to selling goods to students. He wanted to join the army, but when they noticed how intelligent he was, they sent him to Uyo Teacher's Training College. Upon graduation, he was able to go to England to study. He didn't let obstacles stand in the way of his education.

I must not forget my headmaster, Mr Kemmer, who recognized my intelligence and encouraged me not to waste my brain. After giving me the opportunity to teach, he gave me the information I needed to apply to WTC, Enugu, and encouraged me to attend.

Teaching is not for everyone. Even my children did

not aspire to teach. Today, everyone is running after money. Being a teacher is not attractive because teachers are not well paid. Some of today's teachers engage in buying and selling to augment their income, so they can survive. They do not give 100% to the job. Teachers aren't even respected in the community anymore. However, I feel as though teaching chose me; that it was my destiny because of the circumstances that led me on this path. I enjoyed teaching because it involves moulding the characters of tomorrow's leaders.

In 1958, after completing my four-year training, I was posted to All Saints Primary School, Rumuokoroshe, in Port Harcourt, to teach primary six pupils. It was a mission school, and the teachers lived in the same compound with the vicar, who later became Bishop Fubara.

One memory stands out to me. Two married men who had children were part of the class I taught. I did not know this until my class monitor mentioned it to me. These men came to school in their uniforms. They were quiet and participated in all class activities. Maybe they were forced to withdraw from school during adolescence. I thought it was commendable that they had returned to school as adults.

George Bernard Shaw is quoted as saying, *'progress is impossible without change, and those who cannot change their minds cannot change anything'.* Nelson Mandela said that education is the most powerful weapon which you can use to change the world. The actions of the two men showed me that people had started to change; they had started to realize the value of education.

Meanwhile, it was around this time that I met my husband.

Chapter 4

MARRIAGE TO HON. DENNIS DIC- FIBERESIMA

Chains do not hold a marriage together. It is threads, hundreds of tiny threads, which sew people together through the years.
- Simone Signoret

December 23, 1957 was a sunny day. The Okrika elites had organized a Christmas dance to mark the end of the year, and the venue was the Okrika Court Hall premises. The dance was to start at 8 p.m. and last until dawn. Having successfully finished my course at WTC, Enugu, I was home on holidays. I was to begin teaching at All Saints Primary School, Rumuokoroshe, in January 1958.

One of the ladies in my village, late Mrs Grace Dennis Adoki, urged me to follow her to watch the dance. I agreed. I vividly remember the dress I wore that day. It was made from white linen fabric with red polka dots.

It had short sleeves, a round neck, and a skirt that flared and stopped below my knees. My figure measured 36" by 24" by 38". It was a simple dress, but the fitting was awesome.

When we arrived at the venue by 9 p.m., the dance had already started. The men conformed to the dress code, which was a suit with a bow tie. Some ladies were dressed in miniskirts and had bottles of Stout on their tables. We sat down at a quiet corner. When Mrs Adoki asked what I would like to drink, I told her Fanta. I sipped that bottle of Fanta until I left. I guess I looked strange because I had not met most of the people at the party before, and I was not used to their kind of social life.

Many men wanted to dance with me, but I politely turned them down. At about 10:30 p.m., I asked Mrs Adoki to escort me to the waterside, so that I could cross over to Ogan Ama. She returned to the party after seeing me off. There the men confronted her with one question after the other.

'The girl that came with you, where is she from?'

'She is an Okrika girl from my village.'

'You are not telling us the truth. She is quite different. Is she married?'

'No. She has just finished her course at WTC, Enugu.'

A man named Dennis Dic-Fiberesima was persistent. When he heard that I hailed from Ogan Ama, he went to see the late Amayanabo of Okrika, Sir S.P.U Ogan, who had been his contemporary at Okrika Grammar School, to enquire about me some more. The king told him, 'She is no-go area, one of the best in my village.'

Dennis was undeterred. He was born into a Christian family on 18 April 1921 in Koronogono, in Okrika Kingdom. His parents were Chief Gilbert Dickens Fiberesima of Iyamakiri and Magdalene Oyiridia Obona Fiberesima, the only daughter of Chief Obona Fiberesima. He attended Okrika Boys' School from 1930 to 1938 and was one of the pioneer students of Okrika Grammar School, which he attended from 1940 to 1944. He was charismatic and fluent in English language, so he became the district interpreter at Degema headquarters from 1946 to 1947 when Europeans were district officers. He was the station clerk at West African Airways Corporation from 1948 to 1952. When I met him, he was working in Port Harcourt with the Town Planning Authority. With the information that he received about me from the Amayanabo, Dennis started to ask for my hand in marriage.

In Okrika tradition, there is a coming-of-age ceremony for girls called *Iria*. Girls aged fourteen to eighteen perform the rites which initiate them into womanhood. It typically begins with a public physical examination of the girls to ensure they are virgins. Their breasts and stomachs are examined to make sure they are not pregnant. Any girl who is pregnant and performs the ceremony would be openly disgraced at the venue by the *egberiereme*, who is the most elderly woman in the community. The girls parade through the community bare-breasted. They can have their chests and bodies painted. After this, they are led to the fattening room.

In the fattening room, they are fed sumptuous food and pampered for about a month to make them plump. Being plump was considered desirable for womanhood and childbearing. Female elders teach the girls folklore and songs about the community. Males don't have access to the rooms. It is believed that girls have romantic attachments to water spirits, which need to be broken before they can marry. To break the romantic ties, they go to the river and sing the songs they have learned while an *osokolo*, a senior male member of the community, beats them with a stick to ward off the spirits. On the final day of the rites, their families celebrate their initiation into womanhood with a party.

The Iria ceremony is an aspect of our culture that preserves the dignity of womanhood. I did not perform the rites because I was pursuing my education and not looking forward to settling down for marriage. I told Dennis that I was not yet ready for marriage but was interested in furthering my education. He was persistent. His visits were unending. I had started teaching at All Saints Primary School, Rumuokoroshe. Since the teacher's quarters was in the church compound, Bishop Fubara was aware of his visits. It took him a year of pleading to wear me out.

My mother expected me to marry a caring husband, and she kept trying to choose a partner for me. She sized my suitors up and dismissed them one by one until my father asked her, 'Are you the one to marry her?'

In November 1958, my parents and my eldest brother gave the go ahead for our marriage. When I accepted

Dennis' proposal, my mother took me aside and said, 'Now that you have made your choice, your destiny is in your hands. You are not coming back home to stay. You are married and have to stay with the man for the rest of your life.'

From my parent's marriage, I learned that marriage could be sustained through love, trust, and care. These attributes enable a husband and wife to stand united for better or for worse. It was a real credit to my father that I never saw him bring another woman home. He did not have a child outside wedlock. Heading into marriage, I knew theirs was a model I could follow.

Our marriage was celebrated at the registry in Port Harcourt on 7 March 1959, and the solemnization was at St. Peters Church, Okrika. My brother, late Elder Stephenson Jones Ogan, represented my parents, and he signed the marriage certificate. We celebrated our marriage according to native law and custom at Ogan Ama. Dennis married me according to the *ya* marital rites of our culture.

In Okrika culture, there are two types of marriages, *igwa* marriage and *ya* or iya marriage. In igwa marriage, the husband has limited rights over the wife, and she and any children of the marriage belong to her family. The children have no inheritance in their father's family. In ya marriage, a wife is bound to her husband forever, even after his demise. To be free, her parents must return double the expenses incurred by her husband in marrying her, and his family must accept it. Then certain rituals need to be performed to secure her release.

Marriage to Hon. Dennis Dic-Fiberesima

So, I could not return to my people, and my children would have no inheritance in my father's house. They are genuine children of their father who can contest for any office and partake of any inheritance in the Fiberesima house. They are the *furo awo* of the house.

At the time we got married, Dennis' parents had passed. Dennis' father had ten children from different mothers. They are, Anderson, Samuel, Dennis, Clinton, Adam, Reginald, John, Sotonye, Stella, and Tamnumopekerebia. Zechariah, Stella's younger brother, returned with his mother to Igboland and never came back.

When Dennis' father died in 1946, the mantle of leadership fell on Dannis. He became the breadwinner and caretaker of both his siblings and his father's widows. His father's wives were Mabel Ayojion, Adam's mother; Itelima, mother of Reginald, John, and Sotonye; Cecilia, she had no children but took care of Stella; and Magdalene, mother of Anderson, Samuel, and Dennis. The mothers of Tamunopekerebia and Clinton were not living in the compound as wives.

Late Chief Gilbert Dickens Fiberesima, Dennis' father, was very sociable and made friends with some European district officers who were his regular guests. He founded an obscure fishing village called Ikpukulubie and when he died, my husband administered the place and stood against illegal claimants. Dennis' vision for Ikpukulubie was to upgrade it to the status of an Ama which he achieved by planning and developing it. He allocated land for schools and churches because he wanted to enlighten the people. He renamed the place Dic-Fiberesima Ama.

Iyamakiri Fiberesima was my husband's grandfather. He founded two compounds and had five children, Andrew (Papa King), Ada, Abalanga, Aju, and Chief Gilbert Dickens. The first compound he founded is known as Iyamakiri compound (Odo). It was given to his son, Chief Gilbert Dickens, as his heritage. It lies in the centre of other compounds, bounded by Mrs Ogan's compound in the east, Sonari's compound in the northeast, the back of St. Peter's Church in the north, the Okrika Boys' School field in the west, and Gream Polo in the southwest. The front gate is located in the south. The second compound is in a new layout located after Reverend Sarki Fiberesima's mother's compound. It was given to Papa King, Abalanga, and Aju and their heritage.

Dennis had a successful career in public service. From 1953 to 1965, he was the secretary of Town Planning Authority, Port Harcourt. It was during this era that Greater Port Harcourt was planned. He was appointed an agent for Trust Properties, Rivers State, and in 1968, he was appointed to the Federal Public Trustees. He was chairman of the Nigerian Society for the Prevention of Road Accidents in 1963. He was once the president of Okrika Grammar School Old Boys Association and chairman of the Setari age group of Okrika for several years. In 1979, he was elected a legislator in the Rivers State House of Assembly under the auspices of the National Party of Nigeria (NPN) where he also served as an executive member of the Rivers State branch. He was a legislator from October 1979 to December 1983.

My husband, Hon. Dic-Fiberesima, Dennis, depended on God for everything. Every speech he made began or ended with, 'By the grace of God'. Funny enough, the Okrika youths nicknamed him, *abaji* grace of God. The word Abaji is a corrupted form of the word 'by' which they used to mock his accent.

When he was younger, he was a member of the choir in St. Peter's Church, Okrika. He was a devout Christian who served in various arms of the church at both St. Peter's Church, Okrika, and St. Cyprian's Church, Port Harcourt. He was a member of the Parochial Church Committee (PCC) and leader of the Steward Guild. He served as harvest chairman at various times both at St. Cyprian's and St. Peter's. As a Synod delegate, he regularly and hospitably hosted several venerable delegates in our house in Okrika.

When the old organ at St. Peter's, which was built in 1929 by our forefathers, stopped working properly, the PCC decided to replace it with a new one. This happened in the eighties. Dennis mobilized the old boys of Okrika Grammar School to raise funds, and it was a huge success. The church appointed five members to take charge of the contributions and directed that they open a bank account with the funds. Unfortunately, for over fourteen years, no account of the funds was given to the church. Being a man of integrity, he woke all that were asleep. To avoid a crisis, some eminent sons of Okrika came to the aid of the church and purchased the pipe organ that the church is using today.

His love for God and humanity prompted him to provide a site for St. Paul's Anglican Church in Dic-Fiberesima Ama for the expansion of the gospel of Jesus Christ. He contacted St. Peter's Church, Port Harcourt, to oversee the young church. Retired Bishop Pepple of the Niger Diocese of the Anglican Communion performed the foundation laying ceremony. This was a dream fulfilled for him. People in the community cherished him for his peaceful disposition and constant exhortation on the need for peaceful coexistence.

On the seventieth birthday of my husband in 1991, we organized a thanksgiving service at St Peter's, and late Bishop Fubara was invited as a guest preacher. While on the pulpit, he revealed how Hon. Dic-Fiberesima, Dennis used to visit his station almost every day to seek Silverline's hand in marriage. There was an uproar of laughter in the church. Later when his age group members came to the house for refreshments, they cracked jokes and teased him about his visits, and the laughter continued.

Bishop Fubara thanked God that Dennis succeeded in wooing me, and I thank God even more. We were married for forty-two years until his demise in 2001.

Marriage to Hon. Dennis Dic-Fiberesima

Jones T Ogan
(My Father)

Eunice Jones
Tamuno-Orunengime Ogan

Elder S.D.J. Ogan
(My Elder Brother)

Hon. Dennis Dic-Fiberesima
(My Husband)

Silverline Dennis Dic-Fiberesima

Silver Linings in Dark Clouds

Dennis & I at our wedding
1959

Marriage to Hon. Dennis Dic-Fiberesima

Dennis & I at our wedding

Hon. Dennis Dic-Fiberesima

Silverline Dennis Dic-Fiberesima

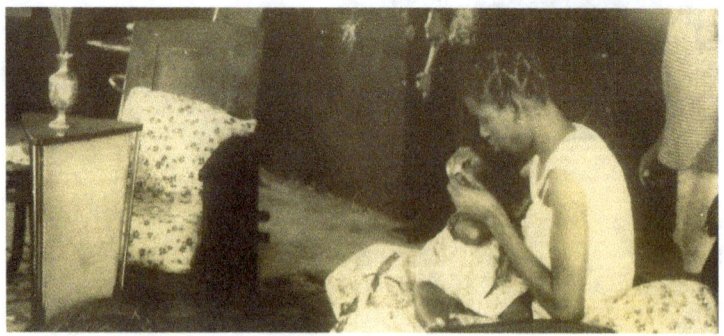
Dakoru & I

Dennis & 1

Marriage to Hon. Dennis Dic-Fiberesima

Receiving a gift from Rivers State College of Education for graduating with distinction

At Graduation from Rivers State College of Education

Chapter 5

A QUIVER FULL OF ARROWS

Lo, children are an heritage of the Lord: and the fruit of the womb is his reward. – Psalm 127:3

My husband and I did not decide the number of children we wanted. We believed God would provide all we needed for the upbringing of the children he blessed us with. We desired to have a female child. We anticipated a girl with each pregnancy, and when the child turned out to be a boy, we continued trying, just in case the subsequent child would be a girl. All my children's births were normal. There was no unusual circumstance surrounded my pregnancies apart from one born prematurely.

After a year at All Saints Primary School, I was redeployed to Okrika Girls' School in January 1959. That year, I had my first baby. He was born prematurely on 19

July at Okrika Maternity Home at seven months gestation. Only midwives attended to the birth. Okrika Maternity Home did not have medical facilities like incubators for premature babies. I was afraid of handling a tiny little baby, and I cried and cried. Late Mrs Grace Isaac Fiberesima, who was an experienced nurse, comforted me. She was married to Chief Dr Isaac Fiberesima, who was related to my husband, and the head of Fiberesima Opukpe war canoe house of Okrika. Her husband usually sought my husband's opinion on critical issues. She was the only one who gave us hope that my premature baby would survive.

She told me that her son, Tunde, was also born prematurely. Every morning, she would massage my son with cod liver oil. Immediately after, she would wrap him up so that only his mouth and eyes were exposed. After I breastfed him, she put him back in his netted baby basket. Within three months, he grew and resembled a full-term baby. It was then I started smiling and being thankful.

One day, I heard a voice telling me what to name my child. The name has twelve letters, but I was instructed to call him by the first six letters only; otherwise, he would be killed. We called him Dafuro, which means 'father's family'. I waited on God for years before revealing his full name, Dafurotibida, which means, 'father's family leader'.

In January 1962, I was redeployed to St. Cyprian's Primary School, Port Harcourt. In November of that year, I gave birth to a boy, and we named him Dikiwarifaka, which means, 'the house properly taken care of does not perish'. God blessed us with another boy in July 1965, and we named him Dumobakateinme, which means, 'life is the greatest of all'.

My mother had contracted asthma while she was at Degema Prison. It persisted all her life, and her condition steadily deteriorated. The constant attacks hindered her from actively participating in Christian activities that involved women and did not allow her to be present for the delivery of my children. My parents lived together in their house at Ogan Ama. Constance Owupelesam, the only daughter of my aunt who died in 1950, fetched water, cut firewood, and ran errands for my mother because none of us, her children, were at home to help.

One Sunday in 1966, my relations visited and told me that my mother's condition was quite bad and that she desired to see me immediately. When I got to her home, there were many church members around who had come to pray for her. As soon as she saw me, she asked them to leave us alone, so that she could talk with me privately.

My mother was a meticulous petty trader. She told me to look in all the nooks and crannies of her room for money that she'd hidden. She did not keep her money in the bank because banks did not operate at Ogan Ama or even Okrika at that time. As a petty trader, she needed her money to buy and sell often. Then she sent me to another room where she had kept someone's money. I asked her if she owed anyone, and she said no. I also asked her if anybody owed her money, and she said no. She talked to me about many things as if she was handing over a mantle to me.

Following her instructions, I counted all the money and gave it to my father. He was astonished that she had such an amount of money. In addition, I gave him the money that someone had given her to keep so he could return it to the owner. My parent's marriage was binding. By that, I mean, they never discriminated; what belonged to one, belonged to the other. My father stood by my mother through her trials, and he was her next of kin.

She told me to take care of my brother's daughters who were living with her, even though one of them was not behaving in a manner that pleased her. She didn't want me to forget my father's family although by marriage, I belonged to my husband's family. She also wanted me to give some of her wrappers to my brother's daughters.

The next Monday morning, I received word that my mother had passed peacefully. My eldest brother was in Zambia. My immediate elder brother could not contribute much. My father was weakened by the sudden separation and preoccupied with thoughts of how he would manage alone. I had to bear the responsibility of burying my mother alone. I was thirty years old. I was a teacher and pregnant with my fourth child.

The constitution of the Ogan Ama war canoe house of the Ado royal family states the rights and benefits accruing to a member of the house at death in article 14, section 1. The family is expected to inform the house chief and chairman of the death of a member. The community is expected to actively participate in the burial rites as a mandatory contribution by commiserating with the family, contributing money, purchasing a casket, and digging the grave. Contributed funds should be given to the next of kin of the deceased member.

Two women from the women's group dressed my mother's corpse. I was directed to put a fathom of *njiri* cloth through her private part to close her womb as part of the burial rites. The community rallied round us during the burial, and my family entertained them with drinks and biscuits.

As for my father, he was blessed with good health. He never took ill. He carried on with fishing after the death of my mother. He did not remarry or have girlfriends. Just before his death on 6 October 1973, he complained of insomnia. My eldest brother had returned to Nigeria earlier in 1971. He buried our father close to my mother's grave at Ogan Ama cemetery in accordance with the burial rites stipulated in the constitution.

After I had organized my mother's burial in 1966, I gave birth to another boy, our fourth son, Damiebi, in November. His name means, 'the goodness of God is great'. When the Biafran War ended, we finally had a girl in 1970. Her name is Dakoru Ine Debokika. It means, 'waiting for the father, mother, and portraying the husband's image', respectively. Then in 1972, we had our fifth son and sixth child, Duabokuro. His name means saviour's power.

People started teasing me that I was delivering children like tilapia fish. Chief Dr Isaac Fiberesima, our family doctor, gave me some injections to prevent pregnancy. However, despite the injections, I had our seventh child on 8 December 1977. We called him Datonye, which means, 'God's will'.

Interestingly, much later in life, it was revealed to me that my late brother, whom I never knew, was always by my side in the spirit, protecting me. He was born to be one of my sons. The name we called the son was also mentioned in that revelation. Please pardon me if I do not disclose it.

I was still pursuing my teaching career when I had my children. After I had my first son, combining the roles of wife, mother, and teacher, was very burdensome. My mother was sick most of the time and could not help me. However, as time went on, by God's grace, I was able to combine raising my children with my career.

We had a good driver from Akwa Ibom State who stayed with us for fifteen years, and he brought us good domestic helps who suited our family. One of them taught me how to extract palm oil from palm kernel. He said that his grandmother was good at it, and he had learned from her. When Dakoru, our daughter, was born, the driver brought a young nanny to take care of her.

The young nanny loved to play. She would rather always carry the baby than do any housework. Sometimes, she would pinch Dakoru to make her cry so that she could rock her and sing to her. One day, Dakoru cried so loud that I came out and enquired about what had made her cry. Then the driver told me that the young girl had pinched Dakoru because she did not want to help prepare things for cooking. I warned her that anytime I heard Dakoru cry, I would severely pinch her. That was how her mischief stopped.

My children started school early. They were brilliant and well behaved except Dikiwarifaka who was unruly during his secondary school days. Many times, I would go to his school to plead for pardon on his behalf. During that period, he was in the habit of insulting his elder brother and provoking him to a fight, boasting that he would floor him. One day, I was in the kitchen when they began to fight. It was serious combat, and I could not separate them. Suddenly, his older brother carried him and put his back on the ground. That test of strength made him sober.

Three of my children had health problems. Dikiwarifaka had asthmatic attacks while growing up, and when my third child, Dumobakateinme (Dumo), was about six, he became very lean, and his stomach bulged out. I took him to the hospital, and the doctor prescribed Alcopar, a very bitter medicine for hookworm. I emptied the powder into a cup of warm water and asked Dumo to drink the mixture. After his first sip, he refused to open his mouth again. When I threatened him with my cane, he drank a little more and started crying. I wiped his tears. Dumo loved eating, so I promised to give him a small packet of chocolate biscuit if he finished the medicine. He did. The hookworm vanished, and he regained his health.

My last child, Datonye, walked at nine months; however, when he turned two, his legs curved outward from the knees, and he became bow-legged. I was greatly concerned, and I took him to Ituru in Enugu State where they used locally made callipers to straighten his bones. We drove to Enugu from Port Harcourt where the roads had been eaten up by erosion and were narrow with deep gullies, which was a serious hazard. The callipers were made of iron and caused Datonye pain without improving his condition, so we removed them.

Next, we travelled to Lagos by air to visit Igbobi Orthopaedic Hospital. By the time we arrived, there was already a long queue of patients, and we joined the queue. The hospital environment was filthy, littered with dirty and smelly bandages and cotton wool filled the gutters. There were no comfortable seats for waiting patients. An elderly lady standing in front of me turned around and asked if I had come because of my son's legs. After I nodded, she said with confidence, 'Go and give him cod liver oil, and the whole problem will be over.'

When the doctor had still not arrived and it was almost time for our return flight, we decided to leave. Back home, I started giving Datonye cod liver oil as the elderly lady directed. Not long after, an Indian doctor who specialized in treating bones joined the staff at University of Port Harcourt Teaching Hospital (UPTH), and we went to see him. He asked me what I was giving Datonye, and when I said cod liver oil, he humorously replied that even if I gave him a barrel of cod liver oil, there would be no remedy. He said the only thing that would heal the bone was vitamin D3, which could be purchased from a pharmaceutical company in Lagos.

My husband took the doctor's prescription to the pharmacy and returned with only three capsules. To administer the drug, we opened one capsule, poured half of the powder into a spoon, mixed it with milk, and gave it to Datonye two times daily for three days. That was how he was marvellously healed.

I believe that motherhood is a divine call to responsibility. Mothers should give their children balanced and nourishing meals, keep them warm, particularly during the rainy season, and ensure they wear clean clothes. It's important to keep all medicines out of their reach, and ensure they do not play with sharp objects. Symptoms of fever can be fatal, so mothers should promptly attend to their children and always deworm them. Discipline is vital. We should correct our children when they are wrong rather than pamper them, so they do not go astray and bring shame on us when the police arrest them for criminal offences.

Finally, if we raise our children in love, not fear, they

will confide in us instead of going to their peers who might misdirect them.

In short, the Bible admonishes in Proverbs 22:6, train up a child in the way he should go: and when he is old, he will not depart from it.

My Children

Dafuro Denni-Fiberesima

Dikiwarifaka Denni-Fiberesima

Dumo Denni-Fiberesima

Damiebi Denni-Fiberesima

Dakoru Denni-Fiberesima

Duabokuro Denni-Fiberesima

Datonye Denni-Fiberesima

Ibi Diki Fiberesima   Boma Diki Fiberesima   Diki Diki Fiberesima

With Dumo's children in Canada

With Dumo's Children

Chapter 6

THE OKRIKA CRISIS

Wa kirike (We are the same)

In 1961, I was teaching at Okrika Girls' School in Okrika, while my husband was working in Port Harcourt, and he came home to Okrika during the weekends.. I lived with my first son and my nine-month-old baby in the family house, which my father-in-law, Chief Gilbert Dickens Fiberesima, built. The house was in Iyamakiri compound. The compound is part of the Fiberesima Opukpe war canoe house of Okrika.

One morning, my baby had a fever, and I carried him to the courtyard because the experienced elders were there, and I wanted to see if they could help. There were no nearby hospitals. Suddenly, we saw people running and learned that they were fleeing attacks by the Konijus.

Okrika has been divided along lineage lines between the Konijus and Tubonijus for a long time. The ancestors of the Tubonijus were mostly traders. They traded with the British and acquired land and bought slaves to increase their manpower. They were wealthy and influential. The ancestors of the Konijus were mostly fishermen. The rivalry between both groups stemmed from contention over the monarchy of Okrika.

Okrika shares boundaries with the Kalabari, Bonny, Ogoni, Eleme, Andoni, and Ikwerre people. Oputubeya is acknowledged as the founder of Okrika, and both the Konijus and Tubonijus claim him as their ancestor. It is said that King Igo, the fifth king from Oputubeya, was killed in a conflict with the Kalabaris. Then the people of Bonny demanded some items either for rituals or to appease them and avert war, but the Konijus could not provide them. Ado of Tuboniju provided the items with the understanding that going forward, the royal throne of Amayanabo of Okrika would be the preserve of him and his descendants. According to the story, this is how the Ado royal house got exclusive right to the Amayanabo throne of Okrika. However, as time went on, the Konijus began to demand a shot at the throne or they would have their own separate king.

The Uwechia Commission of Inquiry was setup in 1959 to investigate the conflicting claims to the throne by the Konijus and Tubonijus. Before the Commission's report was released, the then Eastern Government announced that the throne would be rotated between them. This was in 1960. Thus, Zedekiah Fibika of the Ado royal house of the Tubonijus became Amayanabo. He died that same year. So the Oputubeya house of the Konijus enjoined the Eastern Government to recognize their candidate for Amayanabo in line with the earlier announcement.

Ado royal house would not agree for Oputubeya house to produce the king. Tensions mounted as claims and counterclaims were made by both houses, and this led to the Okrika Crisis of 1961.

That day, during the confusion and panic, the attacking Konijus reached our compound. I belong to the Tubonijus; therefore, I was a target, and my husband's family belongs to the Tubonijus, so they too were targets. I ran upstairs with my baby, and the assailants followed me. They commanded me not to touch anything, and I begged them to allow me collect my feverish baby's blanket to cover him up, but they bluntly refused and walked us out. The atmosphere was tense. I ran to the house of a pastor and teacher who was not from Okrika, but from Nembe, to shelter my two children and me. His house was close to ours. They later came to the pastor's house and commanded him to give us up, they tried to terrorize him, but he told them that they would have to kill him first. Since he was not from Okrika, they left him alone and walked away.

We stayed in his house until evening when the police

arrived to take control of the situation and by then, my baby had started convulsing due to cold. When the town was a bit calm, we were led to late Thio Kalio's house. Thio Kalio belonged to the Tubonijus, and he was married to a woman from the Fiberesima house. We passed the night in his house so that in the morning, I could go to Port Harcourt in his boat as I had no money on me. That night, my baby died.

Meanwhile, my husband, who at that time was a timber merchant alongside his job, had travelled to Opobo to oversee his business operations. Opobo lies east of Bonny in the Niger Delta. After he finished his business, he headed towards Okrika unaware of what was happening. When he got to Dikibo Ama, a man shouted his name and told him to turn back to Port Harcourt because Okrika was on fire, and if he entered Okrika, they would kill him. He turned around and headed for Port Harcourt.

The following morning, Thio Kalio took us by boat to Port Harcourt where my husband was anxiously waiting. Mrs Fubara, popularly called Mama Fubara, was a Nembe woman who had a child called Patience. Patience married an educator and pastor, Mr Samuel Amadi, from Amadi Ama in Okrika. Patience was the renowned headmistress of Port Harcourt Primary School, which was highly esteemed by parents and pupils. Mama Fubara was a close neighbour, and we lived opposite one another on Bathurst Street. When I got to our house with my dead child, I was devastated. My neighbours rallied round me and took the dead child from me. Mama Fubara, out of pity, brought clothes for me and urged me to remove the ones I had been wearing which I had used to carry my dead child.

Given the situation, I could not refuse to wear another person's clothes, so accepted her offer and thanked her immensely. They quickly went to Port Harcourt cemetery and buried the child.

The 1961 Okrika Crisis rendered many people homeless with properties vandalized and innocent lives lost. The huge loss drew the attention of government, and at the end of 1962, Mr R.T. Graham, an administrative officer in the service of the Eastern Government, was appointed to conduct a commission of inquiry into the recurrent outbreaks of violence at Okrika.

The Graham Commission's report was published in 1963. It noted that the fundamental cause of violence was the dispute over the Amayanaboship. The report recommended among other things, that the Ado House, composed of Abam, Dokube, Ibanichuka, Fibika, and Ogan families, be recognized as the Amayanabo House of Okrika, from which the Amayanabo of Okrika should be chosen.

The 1961 riots had begun with massive looting but later escalated to setting buildings on fire and killings. Our house at Okrika was looted and burnt, and my mother-in-law's compound was also destroyed.

Dennis single-handely rebuilt the houses and reinstated all his relations. He also assisted some of the children of his helpless relations, creating unforgettable moments in their lives.

Dennis loved oneness and peace. He was concerned about the unity of Okrika, and he stood firm against the pressure group that wanted Okrika to be divided. He assured Governor Okilo's administration that Okrika is an indivisible, integrated nation having one language, one culture, and destiny. The Government secretly sent emissaries to Okrika to see which areas belong to the Tubonijus and Konijus and to investigate the possibility of dividing them. When they landed at Okrika, they asked late Stanley Lazarus to lead them round. He took them to all the biris (quarters) that belong to the Tobonijus and Konijus. Thus, Edeme biri, Awolome biri, Engeme biri, Bulome biri, Ayongu biri, Ededeme biri, Amanonguma biri, Ambeme biri, Agba biri, Egweme biri, Tomo biri, and Koronogono. The emissaries discovered that one biri meanders into another. They were so interwoven; it was impossible to draw a straight line of division. The Government then consequently respected the views of Hon. Dic–Fiberesima, Dennis.

In the year preceding the Okrika Crisis, my husband had lost his eldest brother, Anderson, who was based in Ghana. Then, the following year, our family home was destroyed, and our baby died. What a devastation! These incidents prompted me to relocate to Port Harcourt, but

I did so with a sense of emptiness. I felt as though I had lost everything.

In hindsight, I learned that if there is life, there is also hope of restoration and survival. Amid it all, God intervened and saved my husband, my first son, and me. I started life afresh. I gradually built up myself, and I started teaching at St. Cyprian's Primary School, Port Harcourt, in 1962.

Okrika is derived from the Okrika word, *wa kirike*, which means, 'we are the same'. It acknowledges similarities in our ancestry and culture and the need for unity against external aggression. Today, by the sure mercies of David, we happily coexist as a unit.

Chapter 7

THE BIAFRAN WAR

To keep Nigeria one is a task that must be done.
        - General Yakubu Gowon

A palpable agitation hovered over us. All was not well. It was 1967, and news of an impending war between the Federal Republic of Nigeria and Biafra dominated the nation. The police had already visited our residence at 11, Bathurst Street, Port Harcourt, several times. We were not sure of what they were searching for. Although they had found nothing illegal, one day, they arrested my husband and detained him at an unknown location.

At that time, Nigeria had gained independence from British colonial rule and was divided into four regions, Northern, Western, Eastern, and Midwestern regions. People from Igboland or Ibo tribe dominated the Eastern Region. The capital was at Enugu, and Lieutenant Colonel

Odumegwu Ojukwu headed the region. Geographically, it was situated in the south-eastern part of Nigeria, bounded by River Niger in the west, the Republic of Cameroun in the east, the northern region (today's Benue and Kogi States) in the north, and the Atlantic Ocean in the south. Port Harcourt, Calabar, and other towns in the Niger Delta like, Bonny, Degema, and Okrika, were part of this region that would come to be known as Biafra.

I went to the police headquarters in Port Harcourt to ask about my husband's whereabouts and find out what he had done. My efforts proved abortive. A friendly, elderly Ibo man, whom my husband had been supporting, came to the house to visit, and I took the opportunity to narrate my ordeal and the efforts I had made to secure my husband's release. He was moved and decided to assist me. Then he took me to the office of the police commissioner, who was Ibo. He spoke to the commissioner in Ibo dialect, telling him how good and nice my husband was. He told him that even though nothing illegal was found in our house after several searches, my husband had been detained in an unknown location.

The commissioner then gave the elderly man a note and asked him to go to Bundu Waterside prison. When we got to the prison, we presented the note to the man in charge. My husband was released and came home with us. A friend of my husband who was Ibo and a lawyer contacted him when he heard of his release. He informed my husband, Dennis, that he had seen his name on a list of people from Port Harcourt and environs who were to be assassinated. Based on this tip-off, Dennis secretly made his way to Lagos. He could not take the children and me along to avoid suspicion. Moreover, he intended to hide for a while, then come back. He never imagined that war would break out.

The Biafran War also called the Nigerian Civil War, officially began in July 1967. The leaders of the Eastern Region wanted to secede from Nigeria and become a new republic called Biafra, while the Nigerian state wanted to maintain the status quo.

At independence in 1960, Nigeria was an amalgamation of about 60 million people belonging to over 300 tribes and ethnic groups held together by a fragile trust with no true sense of national unity.

In 1966, Ibo military officers led a coup that overthrew the civilian government, killing the prime minister and the premier of the Northern Region, both of whom were from the Northern Region. Some military officers of northern extraction were also casualties of the coup. The President, who was Ibo, was out of the country on vacation. Although there were also fatalities from other tribes, the suspicion that the Ibos had targeted northerners lingered. Later that year, a countercoup led by officers from the Northern Region targeted officers of Ibo extraction, including the Head of State, Major General Aguiyi Ironsi. Following that, northerners began a pogrom against the Ibos living in the Northern Region. Those who survived fled to their homes of origin in the Eastern Region. The Ibos felt that the Nigerian government, headed by General Yakubu Gowon from the Northern Region, wanted to exterminate them.

The Biafran War

In the faceoff that ensued between the Federal Government and leaders of the Eastern Region, accusations were flung back and forth. Attempts to broker a resolution failed.

To satisfy the clamour of minority tribes in all regions for greater self-determination, the Nigerian government created twelve states out of the existing regions. The Eastern Region was divided into South Eastern State, Rivers State, and East Central State. The Ibo majority of the former Eastern Region were in East Central State. Port Harcourt, Okrika, and other towns in the Niger Delta became part of Rivers State.

However, this was unacceptable to the leaders of the defunct Eastern Region. On 30 May 1967, Lieutenant Colonel Odumegwu Ojukwu declared the region the independent Republic of Biafra, with him as head of the new country. Under this cloud of distrust, war broke out.

***

Earlier on in 1960, Dennis had gone to Ghana to see about bringing his brother's corpse home. I was not in a good mood, and thoughts about our future occupied my mind. Dennis was very involved with the affairs of his extended family, and we were still living in the house his father built. He was not even thinking of building his own house. He didn't have a savings account, only a current account. Sometimes, he would make a reasonable amount of money, but it would be gone within two weeks because he would have spent it on other people's problems.

It was around this time, in 1960, that I heard a voice say, 'Go to your father's compound and build a house. If the worst comes to the worst, carry your children there.'

I was not anticipating anything bad. However, it was the second time I had heard a voice like that, the first time being the instruction about naming my first son. I obeyed because I believed it was not an ordinary voice.

Teachers' salaries were meagre, but things were cheap. I was lucky that my husband never asked for any money from my little earnings. Perhaps he felt that taking money from a woman was an affront to his ego. He believed that feeding, clothing, education, and shelter were his responsibility. So I saved the little I had. Little drops of water can make a mighty ocean.

I could not build immediately; it took me four years to put things together. During that time, a problem became an opportunity. One of my parent's neighbours started dragging the piece of land where my mother planted vegetables and pineapples with them. When my father told me about it, I told him that I would put up a building on that parcel of land and end the contention. He thought I was joking.

I sent an Ibo mason named Oji, who lived in our Iyamakiri compound in Okrika, to my father's compound in Ogan Ama to start building the house. At last, in 1964, I completed the four-bedroom bungalow, and my parents could not believe it.

Mouths started wagging, calling my husband the best man that the community had ever seen because he put up a building for his wife within a few years of marriage.

My husband was shocked when people started congratulating him for such a noble act. When he eventually saw the building, he wondered how I managed to put up such a structure. I reminded him of what he had said when I gave him my first salary after our wedding, 'I have nothing to do with a woman's money.' Well, 'woman's money' built the house.

My father called the chairman and the elders to perform the *okolobapiki* ceremony, a ceremony that endorses ownership. It confirmed that the land on which I had built belonged to my parents. I am naturally unassuming, so I did not give the impression that I built the house.

***

Meanwhile, two weeks after my husband's escape to Lagos, someone put up a notice at our residence. The notice demanded immediate payment of water and land rate; otherwise, the property would be sold within three days. I went to the Port Harcourt local government headquarters at Moscow Road to complain that my husband was away, and I was unable to pay the stipulated amount within three days. The man I saw told me that the order came from the court and not their office. He explained that the notice was a court judgement. Following his explanation, I had no choice than to withdraw the said amount from the bank and make the payment.

That Saturday, I went to Town market, which was close to the Police Children's School, behind Lagos bus stop. When I returned home, my first son gave me a letter someone had asked him to keep for me. The letter said I was to proceed to Okrika Girl's School with immediate effect and report for duty on Monday morning.

I was teaching at St Cyprian's Primary School, so immediately I went to St. Cyprian's Church premises to enquire about the transfer from our headmaster, late Mr Ashiri, and he told me that he had no knowledge of the transfer. I met the vicar of the church, late Venerable Alasomuka. He too asserted that he was not aware. I asked for his advice, he thought about it for a while and urged me to go because my husband was not around. News of war was gaining momentum. He thought it was better for me to die among my people than to remain with the children in Port Harcourt.

On Sunday evening, my children and I left for Okrika Waterside en route to Okrika with our belongings. The Biafran militias had taken over the Waterside, and they refused to let us leave Port Harcourt. An Ibo man called Wokeocha, who knew me, pleaded on our behalf, and then he showed them the transfer note before they yielded.

The following day being Monday, I reported for duty at the office of the headmistress, late Mrs Salome Ateli. She welcomed me with much delight and allocated a class to me. She also arranged working materials for me.

Recall that our family house at Iyamakiri compound was burned down during the Okrika Crisis of 1961, and my husband had not yet rebuilt it. So my only alternative was to go to Ogan Ama and reside in the house I built.

Thus, the revelation, which I had received in 1960 urging me to go to my father's house and build so that I could bring my children there if the worst happened, was fulfilled seven years later. Hallelujah, praise the Lord!

The Psalmist said in Psalm 16:7, 'I will bless the Lord, who hath given me counsel.' I believe that the revelation and the mysterious transfer letter represent God's divine direction in my life. I wondered then, and I am still wondering what would have been our fate if we had remained in Port Harcourt. What if the transfer note that came from the Throne of Grace, which none of the authorities could explain, did not get to me? But more importantly, what if I hadn't obeyed the Spirit of God's revelation and instruction? I now realize how wonderful and mighty God is to those who love Him. Brethren, man cannot comprehend His ways. The love and mercy that He has showered on me is most profound.

By Thursday, a circular was issued to all schools ordering their closure. The war had started. From that day, there was no more movement from Port Harcourt to Okrika. I had emptied my bank account few days to our arrival at Okrika to prevent the family house in Port Harcourt from being sold, and schools were now closed, meaning no salaries. When I arrived at Ogan Ama, there were already six people living in my parent's house: my father and my brothers' children. My children and I brought the total to eleven. I shivered as I wondered how we would fare.

The atmosphere in my community before the onset of the war was very tense. We could not get news about

Nigeria from any Nigerian radio stations. Perhaps the signals were blocked. The British Broadcasting Corporation (BBC) reported news about Nigeria, and Radio Biafra broadcasted false news about the war situation. People were confused about whether to believe the BBC or Radio Biafra.

My grandfather's compound is close to the seashore, directly opposite the eastern part of Okrika Island, and it is always cool and airy. The community built a resting place at the waterfront, using coconut palm trunks as seats. People would gather there to get information and crack jokes with one another. The Biafran soldiers did not allow the men to go fishing or to engage in any meaningful livelihood. Anyone caught was instantly shot. Therefore, the men became housebound. Women became breadwinners because the soldiers permitted them to fish or engage in trade. The men made fun of their plight, especially during Elelenwo market days. Around 3 p.m., when the women were expected back home, they would say to one another, 'Our husbands will soon return, let us go and warm soup and make garri, and keep the house in order.' Then they would leave the waterfront and go home.

To make sure that we had food to eat at home, I accompanied the women in my village to the bush market to buy food items to resell. Movement was restricted. We joined the big lorries that carried passengers and foodstuff along Eleme route to get to Bori, Khana, and Ika, which were neighbouring towns and villages, to buy crayfish. We resold the crayfish at Elelenwo market. And whenever transport was scarce, we would trek.

Elelenwo market was located near a waterside, and it held every five days. It was as boisterous as today's Oil Mill market in Port Harcourt. The Ibos came in their numbers to buy fish and crayfish.

The Biafrans found everything about Nigeria loathsome. They stopped using Nigerian notes and printed theirs. However, because they could not mint coins, Nigerian coins were allowed. Anyone who refused to accept Biafran currency faced serious trouble. I saved Nigerian coins, which I received as change, and used only Biafran notes to purchase items because their currency was not tenable anywhere else. That was how I accumulated Nigerian coins, as I knew, from listening to the BBC that the Biafrans would lose the war, and their currency would become illegal. Trade was very lucrative. From my profit, I purchased foodstuffs and our other needs. In this way, Jehovah Jireh took care of us, and we did not feel the full impact of the war.

As the war progressed, the Nigerian military began to capture Biafran territory. Nigerian soldiers were sent to guard the Port Harcourt Refining Company (PHRC) at Alesa Eleme, which was commissioned in 1965. The refinery is opposite Ogan Ama. Some of the soldiers drifted into our community. They started going from house to house, forcing women out at gunpoint to satisfy their sexual urge. Married women were not spared. The soldiers captured them by force from their homes in the presence of their husbands. Since the men had nothing with which to fight back, they condoned the insult.

Unknown to me there was a certain major, (I will not release the name of his battalion), who had instructed his soldiers not to touch me because I was his. One day, he came to our house and asked me to follow him.

'Follow you where? Please I am married, and I have children, so I cannot follow you,' I politely replied. He frowned and left. My father was present when this happened. He observed our discussion, but was silent. The major came a second time and requested that I follow him. My father's presence bolstered my courage. My upbringing and my marriage oath were at the forefront of my mind. I maintained my stand and refused to go with him. Then my father broke his silence and pleaded with him. He asked him if we could get a woman for him because I was married, but major said no and left.

Just as the fly referred to in the African proverb that says, 'a stubborn fly follows the corpse to the grave', the major was unrelenting. He approached me a third time at about 9 p.m. He urged me to follow him. I stood my ground and refused. On hearing my response, he became enraged, his body vibrated with emotion as he threatened to shoot me dead if I refused to follow him the next time he came round. Then he left.

I knew from his disposition that he had not made an empty threat, but I didn't know what to do. I just knelt by my bed and let the tears that carried my pain flow down my cheeks. I prayed this simple prayer to the Defence Attorney of the universe, 'O God, if you allow this man to shoot me dead for obeying your commandment, then take care of my children.' Convinced in my heart that God had answered my prayer, I slept off.

Early the next morning, the soldiers in the village started packing their things and when people asked them why they were leaving, they said that at midnight, the major had received a signal to go to where the fighting was intense and had been shot dead there. Before daybreak, another signal had come for them to vacate Ogan Ama immediately. Oh, the great works of God! Who can comprehend that I would be alive to tell the story?

When the war began, my children were eight, five, two, and seven months old. They did not feel the impact of the war. Each market day, I brought sufficient food home, and they ate well. Bombs did not fall in our compound. Whenever they heard bombs, they would take cover and make fun of the last child to duck, and that child would run and hide under the bed.

During periods when the battle was particularly fierce, we would hear ceaseless bomb blasts from the refinery site. One day, the blasts were more pronounced and debris from exploding bombs was flying around and hurting people. Our entire community ran into the church for refuge, since the church building was not built to shelter us from bombs, but in faith, we believed that bombs could not fall on the sanctuary of God. We cried and prayed to God to save our land, children, lives, and properties. The community elders made a pledge to God that if he preserved our community, we would honour him by rebuilding the church, and that our generations shall serve and worship God.

In January 1970, after two and half years of war,

Ojukwu, the Head of State of Biafra, fled the country with his family, while the head of the Biafran army, made the surrender announcement. The war was over. Major General Yakubu Gowon accepted the surrender and said that it was a victory for national unity. He said there was no victor or vanquished, and that it was time for reconciliation, rehabilitation, and reconstruction.

The Nigerian soldiers were motivated to go the extra mile to close all loopholes and ensure that Nigeria remained one. During the war, every community in Okrika had supporters of either Nigeria or Biafra, and Ogan Ama was not left out. The soldiers embarked on another mission after the war to fish out people who were on the side of Biafra, and soldiers from Okrika main town crossed over to Ogan Ama to arrest those who had supported Biafra.

Paramount in the minds of people during the war was their survival, and people tended to support the side that guaranteed their safety. Some supported both sides at different times to avoid being killed. The ordinary man's opinion concerning Biafra and secession was not sought before the war, as J.P. Clark put it in his poem, *The Casualties*, 'thousands are burning that have no say in the matter'.

The women could not bear to witness the arrest of their fathers, husbands, brothers, and sons. They knew that if the soldiers had their way, half of the community would be affected. My community has a women's group that oversees the affairs of women. The executives of the group liaise with the chiefs and council of elders in the administration of matters that concern women. Madam Lucy Nathan Ogan, who was the woman leader at that time, came to our rescue.

She mobilized the women quickly and informed them of her plan to celebrate the soldiers' victory in a bid to save our men. The women looked for Nigerian coins with which to appease the soldiers since Biafran currency had become illegal tender. The government later ordered that all Biafran currency be deposited in bank accounts to avoid them becoming worthless. Afterwards, everyone who complied received twenty pounds regardless of how much they had deposited. When the women approached me, I joyously gave them some of the coins I had saved during the war.

These brave and compassionate women used the money collected to welcome the soldiers, thanking them for their brilliant performance during the war and for rescuing the inhabitants of our community. They poured so many encomiums on them that the soldiers were overwhelmed. They left without hurting or arresting anybody. Nobody betrayed anyone. We acted as though everyone had supported the Nigerian forces.

As soon as the war was over and the community safe, every son and daughter of Ogan Ama was asked to contribute towards the rebuilding of the church. Elder Ezekiel Uwakwe Ogan, popularly called Papa Ukwu, reached out to sons and daughters of Ogan Ama who lived in distant lands to contribute. To the glory of God, a bigger and more beautiful church was promptly built.

Every year, our community celebrates Covenant Day

during the second week of July. We come together to thank God for preserving us during the Biafran War. We fast, pray, and participate in various activities. At the end, we have a memorable thanksgiving service.

Reflecting on this sad part of our history, one lesson I would like to pass on is that we should be content with what we have and never violently take what does not belong to us. 1 Timothy 6:7 says, 'For we brought nothing into this world, and it is certain we can carry nothing out.' Nigeria was under British colonial rule when our leaders asked for independence, and it was a gradual process handled with maturity, and it peacefully yielded results while Biafra's leader, Lieutenant Colonel Odumegwu Ojukwu, was in too much of a hurry and unilaterally seceded from Nigeria, resulting in war. To actualize their secession plan, the Biafran leadership ordered arms and printed their own currency. They carried out internal cleansing against influential indigenes of the region who were not in support of their ideologies. My husband was a target, and many innocent lives were lost, properties worth billions of naira were destroyed, time and resources were wasted, and children suffered from kwashiorkor, all to what end? In the end, Ojukwu's ambition was crushed.

In the light of the above, the recent call for secession by the Biafrans when the economy is in recession with high rates of unemployment and high cost of living, and at a time when business and industrial activities have slowed down, does not make sense.

The Yorubas, for example, have focused on education, culture, language, music, trade and industry, arts, films, and so on. They are advancing in all spheres of human endeavour and making Nigeria great. Let each tribe in Nigeria borrow a leaf from them, and bury the fruitless ambition of trying to colonize others. It is better to use our energy constructively rather than destructively. A Nigerian proverb says that kola nut is grown in the west, eaten in the north, and worshipped in the east. It is better to focus on the things that unite us.

The war changed me. I witnessed the fruitlessness of devastation. I will always advocate for peace in every situation.

In 1969, Port Harcourt was liberated. People were free to move about, but the Nigerian soldiers were on alert to forestall any uprising. They combed for arms and detonated bombs. By this time, we had been totally cut off from my husband as we had no means of contacting him. He returned to Port Harcourt as soon as it was liberated and moved us from Ogan Ama.

Chapter 8

LIFE AFTER THE WAR

You are never too old to set another goal, or to dream a new dream. - C.S. Lewis

After Port Harcourt was captured and the Biafran soldiers disarmed, the Ibos abandoned all they had acquired and ran for their lives. They didn't even lock up their properties and many of them died trying to flee. The indigenes in the city were certain that the Nigerian side had won the war because Port Harcourt was a stronghold of the Biafrans and they welcomed the Nigerian soldiers with great jubilation and started gathering the spoils of the war. This led to a popular saying, '*a capture me a furuke*,' meaning, 'I only captured; I never stole'.

Eventually, Rivers State government declared that the properties deserted by the Ibos were abandoned properties and confiscated them. Many Ibos who returned after the war did not have the proof required to claim their properties and were dispossessed of them. My husband returned to Port Harcourt immediately it was liberated. He moved us from Ogan Ama to Port Harcourt in 1969, disclosing how he had spent sleepless nights thinking about us. He wondered how I would manage with the children because schools were closed, and I was not earning a salary. He was worried about our safety and concerned about our survival amid war.

He had lived with his elder brother, Samuel, at 85 Igboshere Road in Lagos. There was no means of communication by road, air, sea, or radio, and we didn't have mobile phones then, so we were cut off from one another. The children were happy to see their father, and Dennis was so excited to see the children looking healthy and well-nourished that he took many pictures of them. The same could not be said of some of our neighbours whose children had kwashiorkor due to protein deficiency during the war.

The family house in Port Harcourt was still available, as I had paid the accrued fees for land and water rates, which the Biafran government had demanded before the war; therefore, our house was not sold. We immediately moved back into our apartment on Bathurst Street. My husband had his office in one of the rooms. He was an agent to property owners.

Port Harcourt was quite safe in those days. The government tried to put things in place. We did not know the fate of the Ibo friends and colleagues we had prior to the war, and we still do not know. We never saw them again.

Rivers State government took over the management of schools from the missionaries after the war in a bid to operate a uniform curriculum and make fees affordable for all. They built more schools to accommodate the teeming population, and they established school management boards for both primary and secondary schools. The boards were responsible for posting teachers to schools, salaries, promotions, disciplinary actions, and school inspections. They liaised with school heads when necessary.

I was posted to Bernard Carr Primary School in Port Harcourt in 1969. The school's facilities had not been damaged during the war, so teachers and pupils resumed normal classes.

In 1972, Rivers State College of Education was established. I took the opportunity to go back to school to acquire more knowledge and improve my status. I was thirty-six and had six kids. I did not get admission through the Joint Admissions and Matriculation Board (JAMB), but by direct entry because I had five credits in one sitting during my training at WTC, Enugu.

My husband was supportive, and I had reliable domestic helps, so I coped as a wife, mother, and student. Most of my fellow students were also married with children. Those of us who had Teachers' Grade II Certificates and were in service were paid our normal salaries. It was a wonderful experience. Professor Tasie headed the college at its temporary site close to Kaduna Street. Later, we moved to the permanent site at

Rumuolumini.

The College of Education ran a three-year program to produce Nigeria Certificate in Education (NCE) graduates who would teach secondary school students. University of Ibadan monitored and supervised the college. It was a three-year course of continuous assessment. The university set the assessment questions and marked the scripts. They made sure students met all necessary conditions for graduation.

After our final exams, I was awarded NCE with credit in Education and distinction in Home Economics. The certificates had the logo of the University of Ibadan. The Vice Chancellor, Professor Tekena Tamuno, and the Registrar, S. J. Okudo, signed them in June 1975.

On 11 March 1978, the college held its first convocation ceremony and presented each of the two candidates that made distinction, Lydia Cookey and I, with volume 1 (A-K) and volume 2 (L-Z) of the World Book Dictionary. Representatives of the University of Ibadan were present. My husband and my eldest brother were present. They were proud of me and rejoiced at the honour I received.

Acquiring additional education changed me a great deal. I realized that what life offers depends on our determination and perseverance. It earned me promotion in my career, and I was given higher responsibilities. It also affected my home. I baked my children's birthday cakes and prepared new dishes that were balanced and tasty. My family was healthy, and everyone eagerly anticipated mealtimes.

In 1975, I was posted to Harbor Road Girls' Secondary School. The school was located at the Wesley Church compound. The motto of the school is, 'In love, serve one another'. The principal then was Mrs Boma Iyagba while Mrs Akparanta, Mrs Bobmanuel, and I were housemistresses. Each morning, we made inspection rounds to ensure the girls had made their beds properly with their bedspread, and that the toilets and bathrooms were clean. We inspected the girls to make sure they had dressed properly. Mrs Akparanta and I taught home economics while Mrs Bobmanuel taught one of the social sciences.

During the war, the soldiers had their way forcibly with most of the young women and girls. One consequence of this was that years after the war, the girls were wild and morally loose. The girls in the boarding house were in the habit of jumping the fence to go to town, and in the process, they got into serious confrontations with the school gatemen. They developed an unwholesome reputation and were called *agaracha* girls. Agaracha means a woman of easy virtue.

The school punished those who were caught. Knowing their background, we, the housemistresses, drew them close and counselled them on the after-effects of running around in town. They could ruin their lives by becoming infected with sexually transmitted diseases which can hinder childbearing, they could get pregnant out of wedlock, and they could be looked down upon as unsuitable for marriage.

As teachers, we were dedicated and treated them

with love knowing that their bad habits were not easy to overcome, but we were also strict with them. That was how we handled the situation and permanently erased the *agaracha* tag that tried to tarnish the image of the school. Gradually, sanity came back; their attitudes and morals changed, they acquired self-discipline, and they concentrated on their academic pursuit.

I believe that teaching is not a moneymaking venture, but a service to God and humanity. It requires diligence and selfless service. The joy and satisfaction of a job well done is like an unending spring of water. Today, the girls are married with children, and whenever they run into me, they stop to greet me, give me a ride, or pay my transport fare. I give God glory for using us to make an impact in the lives of the girls. They usually say that the teachers of today are not like us.

In 1982, Rivers State College of Education began to offer degree courses. By then, I had seven children. Since I had a good driver and domestic help, I felt I could cope with returning to school. At the college, there were other older students too. It was an excellent opportunity for us married women with children to further our education. The college was in town, so we didn't need to travel and leave our families. I wanted to make up for the schooling opportunities I had lost and motivate my children to reach for the highest levels of education. They all did, except one.

I registered for a Bachelors of Education course, which I completed in 1984. I graduated with second-class honours in Education, Home Science, and Management.

Acquiring more knowledge led to promotions and new appointments with bigger responsibilities in school administration. My certificate was issued with the logo of the University of Ibadan.

In 1985, I was posted to Enitona Boys High School, Borokiri, Port-Harcourt. The motto of the school is, 'for God: for our country, we live'. The principal was Mr Adolphus Okujagu, and some of my fellow teachers were Mrs Adline Orisa and Mr A.A. Imabibo, who became a barrister.

I headed the Home Economics Department, and the boys enjoyed the practical lessons. The Agric Department introduced school farms where students cultivated seedlings in beds and ridges. During this time, I developed an interest in farming. I began to plant palm seedlings in my compound at home. The school environment was conducive for learning, and the gatemen would not allow the boys to go out until break time.

At Enitona Boys High School, I was a subject teacher on grade level 12. In 1990, I was posted to Archdeacon Crowther Memorial Girls School (ACMGS), Elelenwo, as vice principal administration and promoted to grade level 14. The school's motto is fidelis in minimis, which means, 'faithful in little things'. The vision of the school is to attain educational, moral, and spiritual excellence, while the core values are faithfulness, diligence, academic excellence, dedication, moral uprightness, and creativity.

When I resumed, the principal, Mrs Patience Obuzo,

welcomed me and showed me the vice principal's office. Everything was in disarray. There were cobwebs everywhere. My first impression was poor because the school is one of the home economics centres in Rivers State. I asked a home economics teacher to send me some girls with cleaning materials. Together, we dusted cobwebs, swept, washed and scrubbed the floor, cleaned the table and bookrack; dusted the books and re-arranged them. We decorated the room with flowers, and it had a new look.

The next day, the principal could not believe her eyes. I did not know that I was under her surveillance for two weeks because she wanted to confirm the good report that she'd received about me from my former principal at Enitona Boys High School. After she was satisfied with my performance, she asked the school board for a sick leave of three months to cure a recurring typhoid fever. The leave was granted her, and I acted as principal in her absence.

Not quite long after I became acting principal, two concerned teachers told me what had been going on in the school. A male teacher had been molesting students, and they had not been able to solve the problem. I asked them to prove the allegation before I could act. So they set a trap. The teacher had arranged to have his way with a student on a Friday, during compound work, at precisely 1 p.m. Two female teachers pretended that they were supervising the work.

The student gave a signal to the teachers when the male teacher invited her to enter his room. As soon as she entered the room and closed the door, the female teachers rushed to the door and knocked, asking him to open the door. He was forced to open the door, and they led the student to my office.

She gave oral and written evidence, which she signed, and I congratulated the brave female teachers. I set up a disciplinary committee with the following terms of reference.

- To get oral and written statements from previous victims, which must be signed.
- To listen to the teacher in question and collect his signed statement.
- To suggest punishment based on the code of conduct law for teachers.

The disciplinary committee compiled the written evidence, report of the investigation, the resolution and recommended punishment, and signed them. The male teacher involved refused to appear before the committee. They submitted the report to me, and I thanked them for a job well done. I made three copies. I sent one copy to the principal of the school, who was still on leave. I forwarded one copy to the secondary school board, and kept one for myself. After two weeks, there was no reaction from the school board, so I went to their office to find out what was happening.

I discovered that the officer to handle the case did not have any knowledge of the report, and the file had disappeared. I reported the case of the missing file and asked if I could submit another copy. They agreed and I did. This time, it was read while I was present.

The board recalled the principal from leave. They asked her if she was aware that such things had been happening in her school. She said that she was not aware until I sent a copy of the report to her. The teacher was dismissed from service. I fought a victorious battle to put an end to the defilement of the students.

Another case that was brought to my attention was one involving the non-academic staff. They had not been promoted for years and had remained stagnant on level one or two. I went to the school management board in Obiakpo local government area and pleaded their case. Their joy knew no bounds when their letters of promotion came.

I planned to retire from service the following year. Towards the end of 1990, the commissioner for education invited me for a discussion. I met Mrs Abrakassa who deputized for the commissioner. She disclosed that some parents had gone to the state governor and had appealed to him to ask the commissioner to stop my retirement so that I could remain at the school longer.

I told her I needed rest and would prefer to go on retirement. I did not disclose to her what I had observed in the school. It seemed that the battle I fought to save the girls from defilement had undermined the egos of some staff members, and their attitude towards me changed. The male staff and the associates of the dismissed teacher were also not pleased. I felt as though my safety at the school could not be guaranteed.

I retired from meritorious service on 1 January 1991. After my retirement, some owners of private schools invited me to take up appointments in their schools. I turned down their offers as I need rest and wanted to take care of my family.

Life is sometimes like a circle. ACMGS was the last school I was posted to, and it was the same secondary school that I missed attending when I finished primary school in 1949 because of ill health. I did not make much of it while I worked there, but looking back, it is as if God wanted my feet to touch the grounds of the school; as if he was determined that I make a difference either as a student or an educator in that school.

Chapter 9

MY HUSBAND'S DELIVERANCE

There is no education like adversity. - Benjamin Disraeli

One of the pivotal moments during our marriage happened when my husband had a stroke and his left hand and leg became paralyzed. In addition, he practically lost his memory when I was about to finish my NCE programme. This was in 1974. We had six children, and our last child was two years old. We did not have a house of our own. Dennis did not have any savings or any money in his current account, and I could not look to any of his brothers for assistance. All medical treatments proved abortive. I was devastated.

Around April 1974, Dennis started complaining about not feeling well. Dr. Mrs. Isemokuma, A Caucasian doctor, married to a man from Bayelsa, was the physician in charge of Dennis' case. She explained that the tests carried out on him were negative, except one that showed that his blood level was a bit low. So she could not prescribe any drug for him. She felt that his case might be spiritual and not medical. His condition had not yet deteriorated to stroke, paralysis, and memory loss.

Given the prognosis, I left school, I left the children at home with our domestic help and the driver, and I moved Dennis to a healing home, where he was prayed for all the time. I had never been to a healing home before, in addition, the prayers did not yield positive results; rather, he grew worse. He had a stroke. With unending tears, I spoke to God as if I could see him face to face. I said, 'God won't you have pity on me? Won't you pity these innocent children? What should I do? I am helpless.'

While we were at the healing home or prayer house, Jonah, who used to work for my husband's father, visited us. He suggested that we try a spiritualist who used herbs to cure the sick. We adhered to his advice and moved Dennis to the Mile One/Diobu area of Port Harcourt, where the spiritualist resided. He was from the Ogoni tribe of Rivers State and was popularly known as Danger. Danger told us that first he would check to see whether it was possible to cure my husband. By the time we got to him, Dennis had completely broken down with stroke, paralysis, and memory loss. Danger instructed his workers to make a fire on the floor, very close to Dennis. He plucked some leaves from his backyard and put them in the fire. The smoke from the fire rose and entered

Dennis' nose and Dennis sneezed. After that, Danger confirmed that he could cure him.

Danger lived in a bungalow that did not have a concrete fence like many of the houses in Port Harcourt. Instead, there was a fence made from sticks that protected his shrubs and roots at the back of the house. He gave us an apartment, which was not furnished, to live in. It had only one metal bed, which was like the beds students use in boarding houses, and two short benches. The doors and windows were made from wood and had no metal protectors as is common in most houses.

Danger did not mix anything for Dennis to drink. Each morning, he would heat an assortment of herbs in a big earthenware pot. He would cover him with a cloth, remove the lid from the pot, and put the pot under the bed. The steam warmed Dennis, until sweat poured from him like water. After that, Danger would hold Dennis up and help him to walk as you would a toddler. The herbal heating and exercises continued until Dennis' bones recovered strength, and he gradually started recollecting himself. Every time the spiritualist's assistants came to our apartment, they would shout, 'E go good!' which is Pidgin English for, 'it will get better'. So 'E go good' became my husband's name while we stayed there.

I stayed with Dennis all the time, except when I went to see the children or needed to go to the bank. When I went to the bank or visit the children, I would leave him under the care of one of the spiritualist's assistants. Our driver Joseph, would come and pick me up and take me wherever I needed to go, and I hurriedly returned.

My husband ate light meals such as *agidi, moimoi,* rice, and boiled yam with pepper soup. Pawpaw and pineapple were his best fruits. I used to prop him up with pillows and feed him, but as he got better, he fed himself with his right hand. None of his brothers or sisters visited him. Only Late Chief Dr Isaac Fiberesima visited him and gave me some money while we were at the herbalist's residence. His cousin, late Ibimina Aju Fiberesima, also visited us and stayed with us for two weeks.

Danger operated in another dimension. People came to him to discover more about their spiritual problems. He had a bottle which he operated like a cinema projector. The bottle was clear and about ten inches high with a circumference of about twenty inches. One night, he brought the bottle into our apartment and told us to look in it. As I looked, a lectern and Bible appeared, and someone who looked like an angel stood close to the lectern and rested his arms on it. He was clothed in white, and his clothes flowed from his head down to his feet, and a man stood by the side. The image remained on the screen for a long time.

Afterwards, I asked him what the image I had seen meant because I did not hear any voice. He told me that they were in judgment, and that was all he could disclose. I marvelled that if a mere man could operate at that level, then what about our God! How mysterious is our God who has infinite understanding of all things.

One morning, Danger said to my husband, 'E go good, today you go walk.' He raised my husband on his feet and continued teaching him how to walk. After about a week, to God be the glory, my husband started walking again.

The Almighty remembered me and sent me help with healing in His wings. He comforted me and wiped away my unending tears and turned my gloomy darkness to light.

I had to stop schooling when my husband fell ill, so that I could bear the burden of looking after him fulltime and my children in absentia. His illness had started around April, and by June, when he took a turn for the worse, I had to move him to the spiritualist's residence. We stayed there for three months until September when he was completely healed by the grace of God. We went back home, and I returned to school.

While I was absent from school, Mrs Ibunge Alamina, my coursemate, copied notes for me and gave them to me when I resumed. I appreciated her kindness. The lecturers assured me that given my continuous assessment results, I had already passed and that I should relax. They gave me all the assignments I had missed, and I completed them. To the glory of God, I was one of the two students who graduated with distinction. My husband attended my graduation, and he was very proud of me.

Dennis started life again with nothing. My brother, Elder Stephenson Ogan, was then the commissioner for education in Rivers State, and I appealed to him for help. With his assistance, the military governor at the time appointed Dennis as a board member of the Aikali Company. The company was based in Lagos but owned by Rivers State government. The board members did not relocate to Lagos to carry out their duties. They only went to Lagos for meetings and assessments when necessary. Dennis worked for the company for about three years before new appointees replaced the old board.

The sickness changed Dennis. Before he took ill, his father's people and their needs were his priority, and he wasn't concerned with building his own house or providing properly for his immediate family. When he recovered, he started thinking of how to build up his nuclear family rather than his extended family.

In 1971, my husband's elder brother, Samuel, who had lived in Lagos for over thirty years, was transferred to Port Harcourt. We left our apartment in the family house for him and moved to a duplex at No. 1, Akomas Street, Old GRA, Port Harcourt. In 1972, the Military Governor, Alfred Diete-Spiff, asked my husband to give up the duplex and relocate to Rumuibekwe Housing Estate. We were to own the property (a two-storey building with a bungalow attached) after we finished paying for it. By 1974 when Dennis fell ill, we had not completed payment for the house.

When Dennis recovered, friends and relations who paid him lip service rallied around him. One of our elderly neighbours, whom we called Mama Green from Bonny, called him and thanked God for his recovery. She said, 'Show gratitude to your wife. She is the type of wife any man would pray to have.' Other people who visited him in the office also thanked God for the kind of wife he had.

He became conscious of the things he had neglected, and in 1978, he started rebuilding our home in Okrika. When he completed the two-storey building in 1980, he dedicated it to God, and handing me the key of the house, he said, 'Darling, I can't thank you enough.' He also made relentless efforts to complete payment for our house at Rumuibekwe Housing Estate.

Before my husband became ill, he didn't acknowledge a woman's contribution to the home beyond housekeeping. As I said earlier, he saw himself as the sole breadwinner. However, his experience during his illness helped him change that perception, and he came to realize that women could be as courageous and prudential as men.

He lived for twenty-seven more years before death parted us. In 2000, he was sick for about six months. Two of our children contributed immensely to his upkeep and helped to purchase his medication. Dikiwarifaka (Dikiwari) and I were at home taking care of him until he passed away on 2 January 2001.

***

Before Dennis died, he had two outstanding cases in court. Since I had the right to administer his assets, I represented him in court after his demise. I had never been in court previously. In fact, all the legal conflicts I experienced occurred after his death.

The first case was with Shell, the oil giant who had

rented our property located at 68 Market Road, Rumuomasi, for forty years. When they vacated the property, they vandalized it and left it bare. My husband sued Shell millions of naira for damages.

After a series of adjournments, which spanned two years, I was eventually called to the witness box. My lawyer had spent time coaching me on court procedures before the court date, and he explained the facts of the case to me and showed me supporting documents such as rent agreements and quit notice. I grew in confidence.

I testified uninterrupted before the judge of the High Court in Port Harcourt, Justice Membre. She put her pen down and listened with attention. The court was silent. I also told the court that my husband had tried to rent the property to other companies, but when they saw the condition of the property, they lost interest. This was a great loss of revenue to us. The court asked me how much I was demanding as compensation for that loss.

I said, 'Just a mere one million naira.'

The court that had been silent roared with the laughter of those present because I had referred to one million naira as mere.

The lawyer who represented Shell was unprepared. He must have taken me for granted as he could not cross-examine me when the judge gave him opportunity. He requested another hearing to cross-examine me. As I stepped down from the witness box, he stood up and shook my hand. He was absent at the next hearing. He asked for an out-of-court-settlement instead, so we settled out of court.

The second case was the Akpajo case. Akpajo town is situated in Eleme local government area of Rivers State. Two refineries and one of the busiest seaports in the country are in Eleme. The elders of Akpajo community had come to my husband in 1962 to ask for three hundred pounds. They needed the money to retrieve their land from a creditor because they had pledged it as collateral, and since they were unable to repay the loan, the creditor was threatening to sell the land. They pleaded with Dennis to help them retrieve the land, and that they would compensate him with part of the land. My husband obliged and gave them the money. They in turn gave him part of the land, as promised.

Dennis then mapped out development plans for the land. He took the plans to Pabod Finance Company to request for a loan. The company declined his loan request but went behind his back and bought the land. They registered it with the land office in Port Harcourt. He sued the company, but two weeks before the case was to be determined, he passed. The trial judge, Hon. Justice Daisy Okocha, passed judgment in favour of Pabod Finance Company.

My husband's lawyer, Sobere Biambo, appealed the judgment. After several adjournments, the Appeal Court ruled the case in our favour in November 2016. The court condemned the role that Pabob Finance Company played in the case. However, Pabod Finance Company appealed to the Supreme Court in Abuja. Sobere Biambo is now a judge. Mrs Consistence Iyare is handling the case. She has submitted a motion for accelerated hearing because the case has been in court for over fifteen years. Soon after my husband's burial and while I was supervising the Universal Basic Education (UBE) programme at Okrika, I stopped by our compound to see the condition of things. This was on 21 April 2001. The place was lonely and quiet, but I saw evidence that some work had been done to lay the foundation of a building. I was shocked and asked the two boys whom I met about it. They informed me that a member of our extended family had asked them to monitor the place. I began to remove the pegs, and they ran to tell her. She came by and rained abuses on me.

I took the matter to the chairman of the Fiberesima Opukpe war canoe house, late Sobere Fiberesima, but he was unable to resolve the issue. My husband's friend, late Stanley Lazarus, advised me to report the incident to the chairman of Wakirike Town Council. Just as she had done when the matter was before the chairman of the Fiberesima Opukpe war canoe house, she ignored the summons of Wakirike Town Council. I took leave from my work at UBE and left for Port Harcourt where I told my son what had happened. I urged him to go to Okrika and see things for himself. By the time he got home, she had dug the foundation. We organized some boys to cover the foundation. Then this family member held her peace for the next ten years.

In June 2011, she went to court to decide a case involving her and some other family members because there was contention over family land allocated to her husband. She included me in the suit, claiming damages worth five hundred thousand naira, for destroying her building materials in 2001. We were in court for six years. In 2017, Chief Dr John Dawaridabo Fiberesima, the house chief of Fiberesima Opukpe war canoe house got clearance from the Okrika Magistrate Court to settle the case out of court.

The chief and his council presided over the matter. They went to the site and saw things for themselves. The cement blocks that the plaintiff said I had destroyed were on her plot of land. They ruled that she should build on the plot of land allocated to her husband, and I was free. I did not have to pay the money claimed for damages, and I was not asked to pay settlement fees. The court accepted the chief's report. Our lawyers prepared a document which we all signed, and the case was struck off.

I had to learn to stand on my own in my husband's absence and fight for what is right. In trying to overcome these conflicts, I learned to always stand for the truth, no matter the opposition and no matter what false witnesses say.

***

When Dennis died, the FM radio station in Port Harcourt announced his call to glory. On Wednesday, 31 January 2001, we held a service of songs at our residence in Port Harcourt. On Friday February 2, his body left the Kpainma Mortuary, Elechi Beach, via boat for Okrika. We made a brief stop at Dic-Fiberesima

Ama. Our son, Dikiwari, was dressed in the traditional don attire worn by chiefs and carried a walking stick. He took a standing position at the front of the boat until they arrived at ATC Beach to show that a notable Okrika son was coming home.

We held a Christian wake at our residence, and then on Saturday, February 3rd, a funeral service was held in his honour at St. Peter's Church, Okrika. People from far and near attended, and the church was full with statesmen, old boys of Okrika Grammar School, members of Setari age group, Dic-Fiberesima Ama community, and Fiberesima Opukpe war canoe house, the congregation, and the bishop and venerable of the Niger Delta Diocese, Anglican Communion. The interment took place in front of our compound. The next day, after the thanksgiving service in his honour, we entertained guests.

I had funeral rites to perform after the burial ceremonies. In accordance with our culture, I remained indoors, and a close relation attended to my needs. I stayed indoors for a few days until the funeral bed on which he lay in state was dismantled by the church. I did not adhere strictly to tradition; otherwise, I should have been indoors longer. A member of the Mother's Union of the church shaved off the hair on my head and body. I mourned for six months, always in white clothing, not the traditional black.

Our beloved husband, father, grandfather, great-grandfather, and elder statesman, Hon. Dennis Dic-Fiberesima, is survived by:

My Children:
Dafuro Denni-Fiberesima
Dikiwarifaka Denni-Fiberesima
Dumo Denni-Fiberesima
Damiebi Denni-Fiberesima
Dakoru Denni-Fiberesima
Duabokuro Denni-Fiberesima
Datonye Denni-Fiberesima

Daso Denni-Fiberesima, born by Patience Titi Reuben from Daka family

Dr. Dinma Denni-Fiberesima, born by Isabella Dappa from Dappa family of Bakana

Diepiriye Denni-Fiberesima, born by Florence Yakiah from Browns compound in Finima, Bonny

Dennis-Ada Denni-Fiberesima and Deinbia Okoromah nee Denni-Fiberesima. The two daughters were born by Iyowuna Obona Fiberesima

Throughout Dennis' life, our Almighty Father upheld us, even when all hope was lost. He shielded us from the wickedness of man. His eyes watched over us through the days of distress, and he was our light in the gloomy darkness.

Chapter 10

MY RETIREMENT FROM TEACHING

Education is for improving the lives of others and for leaving your community and world better than you found it.
- Marian Wright Edelman

I was was not in any political party, and I never looked forward to any political appointment, so it came as a surprise when I was appointed a supervisory councillor for education in Okrika local government in 1998. The head of service was Dr Mrs Ipalibo Banigo under the military administrator of Rivers State, Group Captain Egwang. Our chairman swore in the following people on 7 September 1998:

Silverline - Dennis Dic-Fiberesima - Education, Youth, and Sports
Deinma Johnson Ogbo   - Health
Charles Dagogo   - Works
Loveday Ajunyomuka   - Agriculture

Mrs. Ada Don Pedro   - Family Support Programme
Before my appointment, an education committee functioned in the local government area and was managed by the primary school board. Mr Emmanuel Ndamioku from the education committee was sent to the board to specify the areas that the supervisory councillor for education would operate to enhance progress and save cost by not duplicating functions.

The council had a guideline for its operations. We were to work with the secretary of the local government area, treasurer, and engineer in charge of works.

The chairman visited all the communities in the local government area, and they submitted lists of the priority projects in their various zones. Based on that, we started making our own assessment. Although we worked tirelessly, our efforts did not yield much result. Corruption like a cankerworm has eaten deep into the fabric of Nigeria, and no sector is exempt.

By the end of our service as supervisory councillors, we observed many anomalies. The council functioned as if it was autonomous. Only the chairman and the treasurer knew the monthly financial allocation, and they deliberately refused to share that information with the councillors. The chairman spent money and withdrew at will for his personal use. Cost of projects were inflated. The chairman refused to appoint a deputy as stipulated in the operational guidelines. It was alleged that the chairman supported a particular political party, so he stopped the councillors from monitoring the election that was held during our tenure. The chairman took more money for security than was stipulated in the guidelines. All this was just a tip of the iceberg.

Working as a supervisory councillor gave me more insight into the pervasive problem of corruption. If we don't address it, future generations will not have resources to live on. I believe that one way to tackle this recurring problem is for the incumbent president to set up high-powered audit panels yearly to investigate the affairs of every sector of the economy for accountability and transparency. The legislative arm should enact laws to severely punish offenders. Accountability must begin at Aso Rock, then the Senate, House of Representatives, State Government Assemblies and Houses, ministries, parastatals, the civil service, local government councils, the military, and police.

If this is done, Nigeria would be ranked among the richest countries in the world. Poverty would vanish, and the citizenry would be proud of their country. We have no devastating natural disasters in Nigeria, yet we are languishing in poverty because of a few self-centred individuals. We need leaders who are brave, who love Nigeria, and want to serve the country.

***

In 1999, the administration of President Olusegun Obasanjo introduced the Universal Basic Education (UBE) programme. To be effective, teachers from each local government area of the states of the federation were to be trained under a Pivotal Teachers Training Programme (PTTP). Rivers State recruited 15 supervisors and 135 tutors who had served the state meritoriously to train selected candidates as pivotal teachers.

My appointment as one of the fifteen supervisors for the programme was unexpected. When I received my letter of appointment from the school board to handle Okrika and Ogu/Bolo local government areas, I was surprised.

The headquarters of the National Teachers Institute (NTI) was at Kaduna State while our state office was situated at the Federal Housing Authority, Rumueme, Port Harcourt. Mr D.O. Yaya was the interim coordinator until May 2002 when F.M.G Nwisagbo took over. The management of the state primary education board was one of the stakeholders of the programme.

For convenience, the twenty-three local government areas of the state were zoned under the supervisors. Okrika and Ogu/Bolo local government areas were classified as zone 3 and were under my supervision. The PTTP zone 3 had its headquarters at Ogoloma. I supervised nine tutors, and they were A.P. Bamson, T.T. Kiri, I. Joe, S.E. Ben-Kalio, Victor T. Alabo, Dakoru Derefaka, G.T. Datoru, G.F. Frank, and A.I. Amakiri.

The first batch of students in zone 3 numbered 84. We followed the same calendar as the state's schools instead of the weekend and holiday contract programmes designed by the NTI in Kaduna. Rivers State was the only state that deviated from the norm because we started the PTTP late and needed to put in extra effort to catch up with other states.

The students were taught core subjects like education,

mathematics, English, integrated science, and social studies. Optional subjects were physical education, agriculture, Christian religion, and home science. We sent progress reports and continuous assessment results to the state coordinator who collated them and forwarded to NTI, Kaduna.

Before the final examination, the students interned for three months. We posted them to all the schools in zone 3. I wrote to the school heads, asking them to serve as mentors to the student teachers. The school heads were to provide leadership, correct their lesson notes, oversee their lesson delivery and use of instructional aids, supervise their evaluation techniques, and advice on how they were to participate in extramural activities, and relate with the community. The mentors were to rate the performance of the student teachers using forms given to them for that purpose. We sent the teaching practice scores to the state coordinator.

The final exams were held at the UBE facility in Borokiri, Port Harcourt, as the situation at Okrika was not conducive. The first batch of student teachers from Rivers State made the top results in Nigeria. Everybody was excited about their excellent performance.

When it was time for the second batch of student teachers to commence the PTTP, we had less students. This was because the management of the state's primary education board complained that they had been using their statutory allocation to run the programme and could no longer bear the burden. We, the supervisors, were using part of our allowances for minor expenses related to the programme because the money allocated for such expenses had not been paid. After a while, even our monthly allowance of fifteen thousand naira was not paid. We were told that there was no money. We could not believe that a state, which received billions as monthly allocation from the federal government, had no money to run the programme.

By the end of May 2002, the 15 supervisors had not been paid their allowances for nine months, and the 135 tutors were owed six months' salary. It was the same situation with the student teachers. The allowance paid was not even commensurate to the volume of work involved, especially for those in the riverine and remote parts of the state. We all worked tirelessly out of our love for the state.

The supervisors, tutors, and student teachers wrote separately to the executive governor of the state, requesting ₦10,125,000(Naira) for supervisors and tutors.

The governor was not sympathetic to our case, and to date, not a kobo of our outstanding salaries and allowances have been paid. Our march to the State House of Assembly was futile because we discovered that our legislators were not interested in ensuring that we get what is due us. They were there only to attend to their needs.

The UBE program was intended to produce three batches of pivotal teachers in each state. In Rivers State, there was no third batch due to lack of funding. Rivers State has had to recruit teachers from other states because there weren't enough qualified teachers in the state. For any project to succeed, there must be proper planning and management of resources. Capable, experienced, and dedicated staff, should be employed to run the project. The PTTP in Rivers State was carried out haphazardly, and it ended up being a disappointing failure. This viable programme, from which other states benefitted, was dead and buried in Rivers State.

As I said, I never sought for any of the appointments. I believe that when God's grace is operating in your life, you will experience favour. Favour connects you to people who can enrich your life or empower you. It brings you out from obscurity to the limelight. You are lifted, but not by your struggles, beauty, status, or achievement. Favour will correct your mistakes.

In the Biblical story of Queen Esther, we see that she obtained grace and favour in the sight of King Ahasuerus more than all the other virgins in the twelve provinces of his kingdom. God made it possible for Esther, an orphan in captivity, to become queen of the Persian Empire after Queen Vashti was dethroned due to her pride, arrogance, and disobedience. The same can be said of Mary, the mother of our Lord Jesus Christ, who was highly favoured. God choose her and lifted her above all the highly placed women in Bethlehem Judea. I see my appointments as a supervisory councillor and UBE supervisor as orchestrated by the special grace of God. The appointments connected me to some highly placed persons who made impact in my life.

***

After my retirement, I was privileged to visit Israel. I

think that many Christians want to go on pilgrimage to the Holy Land to see where our Saviour lived and get more understanding of the stories and places referenced in the Bible.

Back then, Rivers State government sponsored pilgrims to Israel, and each pilgrim received an allowance of 1,000 dollars. People clamoured for an opportunity to go on pilgrimage. I did not clamour to go. Someone put my name on the Okrika local government list, and my name also appeared in the Rivers State government list. That was how fate prompted me to go to Israel. Three batches of pilgrims made the journey from Port Harcourt to Israel, and I was among the second batch of About 592 pilgrims who were sponsored.

To qualify for the journey, I swore an affidavit before the Commissioner for Oaths at the Magistrate Court Registry, Port Harcourt, that I would return to Nigeria. Failure to do so would cost my guarantor 2,000 dollars, being cost of repatriation. My guarantor was Rev. Michael G. Toby, who was the secretary of Rivers State Christian Pilgrims Welfare Board (RSCPWB). I got a Christian pilgrim's passport and was given yellow fever and malaria inoculations.

We left Port Harcourt International Airport en route to Israel on 6 December 2002. Our flight was smooth. We arrived at Tel Aviv Airport the following day at about 11:30 a.m. and rode in a bus to the Nigerian Embassy then we checked into the Holiday Resort Hotel. I shared room 417 with my partner for the trip, Diepiriye Minawari. The walls of the room were white, and the floor was green.

Our first stop on Sunday, 8 December, was the Sea of Galilee, which was called Sea of Tiberius (John 6:21) or Lake Gennesaret (Luke 8) in the Bible. It is also known as Lake Kinneret. Our bus driver's name was Moses, and Dafni was our escort. Rev. Michael G. Toby was the coordinator of our group.

The Sea of Galilee is a freshwater lake that lies about 200 metres or 650 feet below sea level, the lowest on earth. It is about 11 km wide, 21 km long, and 43 m deep. The lake is the major source of water in the area. St. Peter's fish, sardines, catfish, and mullets, are some of the fish species found in the lake. Many fruits and vegetables are cultivated in the green areas around the lake, which is surrounded by highlands, including the Golan Heights. The mystery boat that belonged to Jesus and his disciples 2000 years ago was displayed at the shore. As we journeyed, we saw olive trees used for producing olive oil, and we enjoyed St. Peter's fish (tilapia) in a restaurant in the vicinity.

We then visited the Mount of Beatitudes which is about 150 metres higher than the Sea of Galilee, yet about 50 metres below sea level. It lies between Tabgha and Capernaum and overlooks the Sea of Galilee, so we had clear views of the lake. The mountaintop is serene. We saw marble stones with the Beatitudes (Matthew 5:1-12) inscribed on them.

At Jerusalem, we prayed for the peace of the city and our country, Nigeria. Jerusalem is the centre of the world, a holy city, and the judgement seat of God.

We were privileged to climb the Mount of Olives from where Jesus ascended to heaven. He will also land there at His second coming (Zechariah 14:4). The mountain is about 800 metres high, so you can enjoy a bird's-eye view of the city of Jerusalem. Many years ago, people grew olive trees on the slopes of the mountain, and that was how the mountain got its name. It is an important part of Jewish history and a burial site.

The Wailing Wall is also known as the Western Wall and it is designated the most holy place of prayer. We learned that King Solomon built the temple on this site. The Romans destroyed it in 70 CE, and the Western Wall is its only remains.

At the border between Egypt and Israel, we were subjected to rigorous security checks. We changed our driver and escort. Reda became our new escort while Ayub became the new driver. The Red Sea is an inlet of the Indian Ocean which lies between the African and Asian continent. It can be seen from the Sinai Peninsula and the port city of Eliat, which is on Israel's southern tip. Its reefs and abundant marine life make it a favourite destination for divers.

Of all the places we visited, the most heartrending for me was the Hall of Remembrance at Yad Vashem on the Mount of Remembrance. It commemorates the Holocaust. It reminded me of a synagogue-like cemetery. An eternal flame burns, and it lights up the dark interior. We saw how the Germans slaughtered six million Jews between 1939 and 1941. We saw sculptures that demonstrated the wickedness of man. They depicted the various ways that people were tortured and executed. A man who lost every member of his family during the Holocaust moulded the sculptures in this historic museum. No one with a soft heart can leave the Hall of Remembrance dry-eyed.

At the end of our exciting trip, Philip Meyer, who was the shepherd representing Israel, awarded us the Pilgrim's Certificate while Venerable Ndewi, chairman of RSCPWB, offered prayers. A parting speech was made at the Banquet Garden, and gifts were given to our escort and driver. Some pilgrims bottled water from River Jordan for spiritual healing. Others collected mud from the Dead Sea for healing and beauty treatment. There were pilgrims who came with their prayer requests and focused on praying. Others who were perhaps business minded bought jewelleries and beautiful crafts.

We checked out of our hotel on December 16th and boarded the plane at 4:30 p.m. We had a smooth flight with a brief stopover in Turkey, where we disembarked from the plane. We took off from Turkey at 7 p.m. and arrived at Port Harcourt International Airport by 12:30 a.m. safely.

It was a privilege to tread the same ground that Jesus walked on while He was on earth. My pilgrimage changed my perception about Bible stories and events. I had imagined the scenes and setting of the stories, but being in Israel made them very real. Indeed, seeing is believing.

Our earthly life is like a pilgrimage. We live for a short time before our exit home. God remains the same forever and ever, and my faith in Him is steadfast.

My Retirement From Teaching

Jerusalem Pilgrimage
at Mount of Olives

At a Mother's Union Conference
at St. Peters AnglicanChurch Okrika

At in-laws wedding ceremony with Dikiwarifaka & Damiebi

With Dakoru

At a Mother's Union Celebration at Ogan Ama

Chapter 11

LEGACY

Let this be recorded for the generation yet unborn, that a people yet to be created will praise the Lord. - Psalm 102:18

I wrote this book because I want my children to know me better. I want them to know about my experiences and trials and to learn from the mistakes I made. I chronicled our family tree because it is important for them to know where they came from. A quote by George S. Patton says that we should prepare for the unknown by studying how others in the past have coped with the unforeseeable and the unpredictable. You don't have to live as long as I have to realize that life fluctuates. Sometimes, we rise, other times, we fall. When we are down, the only one who can sustain us is God, not man. My husband experienced this when he fell ill. Close relations and friends abandoned him. They stayed away when he needed them the most. At all times, our trust should be in God.

My typical day starts with my morning devotion. I praise and worship God, and I read and meditate on a portion of the Bible. Then I pray, asking for God's counsel and guidance. I ask God to help me plan my day and to strengthen me to accomplish my tasks for the day. I ask Him to send helpers to help wherever I may need it. I also present my children to God and ask that His grace, mercy, peace, and comfort, be upon them.

I do not like to procrastinate, and I tackle issues as they come. I keep busy by cooking, sweeping and mopping my home, and caring for the plants in my garden. Work is a form of exercise, and it diverts my attention from burdensome thoughts. I don't like things haphazardly done, so I work on projects and other issues that I am handling. I like learning, so I pay attention to my environment; observing things around me, and I listen to the radio. In my lifetime, I have seen different types of phones, from the rotary dial landline telephone to today's mobile phones. My current phone has features that I am not familiar with, and I take time to learn about them. I enjoy reading my Bible pamphlets.

One of the things I long to see in my lifetime is the eradication of corruption in Nigeria. I witnessed corruption when I served my state in different capacities. I believe it is the root of all the problems Nigeria faces. Most Nigerians love money more than life. They can go any length to acquire wealth like falsifying documents, inflating project costs, embezzling resources, allowing the importation of substandard and illegal goods, arming robbers and kidnappers with information, and participating in ritual murder.

Changing our value system is important if we want to end corruption. A good name is better than ill-gotten wealth. Good deeds cause one to be immortalized in the minds of people. We will be remembered for what we did whether in politics, government, music, art, education, or social services. The dictionary defines legacy as something left or handed down by a predecessor. Our parents and grandparents before them founded villages and compounds and left houses for us. However, the values they handed down to us helped us enjoy the things they left behind for us.

Many people know that the things they are doing are bad, but they still take pleasure in doing them. The Bible teaches that everyone must account for his or her deeds, whether good or bad. The bad things we engage in, which give pleasure, will eventually turn to bitterness just as in the case of the teacher that was caught defiling students. He was dismissed, and he lost all his benefits and entitlements, including gratuity and pension.

Sometimes, we are our worst enemies when we refuse correction. Some youths refuse to go to school or further their education. They go after women or men, go to clubs, drink, and smoke. They gradually head down a path of destruction. In future, their mates will be ahead of them, and they will not be equipped to face the challenges of life. What is also tragic is that these irresponsible persons have children indiscriminately, and these children receive no proper upbringing.

Another measure that can be taken to eradicate corruption is ensuring that those caught are arrested, tried, and sentenced to long jail terms. This measure will require a government that does not pay lip service to the problem.

The Chinese philosopher, Confucius, is quoted as saying, 'By three methods we may learn wisdom: first, by reflection, which is noblest; second, by imitation, which is easiest; and third by experience, which is the bitterest.' One of the mistakes I made had to do with making choices about marriage. Like me, many people, in choosing whom to marry, focus on finding out about their potential spouse's behaviour, likes and dislikes, friends, achievements, religion, and so on. They fail to find out about the background of their family. What traditions are prevalent, and whom do they worship? What customs and rules govern the community from where they hail?

I naively thought that every family was like my family who only worship God. Some families, perhaps out of ignorance, worship water spirits and make sacrifices to them. I believe that these practices create foundational problems that continue for generations. The spirits expect the ancestor's children to continue the tradition of worshipping them.

One good thing that the missionaries did was introduce Christianity to us. We have come to see that idolatry is bad. It hinders the prospects of adherents and their children. Their destinies end up being twisted, and only by the grace of God can they be rescued from all these problems.

If I were to sum up my life in three words, they would

be, unassuming, dedicated, and courageous. However, I am not perfect. Each of us has good and bad sides. Only God is perfect. I tend to brood over ills done to me, and I have a temper. When I am angry, I talk loudly as though I am shouting. I am not sociable and have no gregarious instinct in me.

I remember once when my husband and I were having a discussion, and he asked, 'What do you know?' I flared up. I told him that he had gone ahead and taken decisions without consulting me. I began to list incidences and quote dates.

He was baffled and exclaimed, 'What! All these months you kept all these in your mind?'

I am trying to overcome by releasing all suppressed emotions that congest my mind. I forget the past and press forward to the future. Although I am not socially inclined, I try to get to know people, and learn to work well with them. I check my anger and try to control it before it rises and gets out of hand. I am seeing improvements, and my angry episodes are gradually becoming less and less.

I have been privileged to handle children all through my life. I have seven of my own and countless more have been a part of my life because of my teaching career. I care about children. I have eleven grandchildren at present, and more are on the way. They are the future. As parents and guardians, we should draw our children close. That way, they will feel free to confide in us rather than their peer groups. If we bully them, we will instil fear in them. It's better to correct them with love rather than to let them grow wild.

We cannot let ourselves get too busy to check on their progress at school, and liaise with their teachers. It is important to get to know their friends and the families of their friends to discourage friendships that are not good for them. Health is wealth. Give them urgent attention at the first sign of fever or any other ailment, ensure they have balanced meals, and provide a conducive home environment for them. In future, they will turn out to be precious jewels for you.

After I finished primary school in 1949, circumstances beyond my control forced me to teach in 1950 instead of going to secondary school. At that time, pupils started school at a later age than they do today. I taught big boys in primary three, and I gave them their due respect. I did not undermine them nor despise them. In fact, we were like equals. Interestingly, Professor Tekena Tamuno, Chancellor of the University of Ibadan, who signed my NCE in 1975, was one of the big boys I taught in that class. That's the irony of life. The future is unpredictable.

Similarly, in 1985, I was posted to Enitona Boys High School. The principal at the time, Adolphus Okujagu, was one of the big boys that I taught in 1950. Venerable Otobo of the Anglican Communion is one of them too. Whenever we meet, they still address me as Ma, recognizing me as their teacher even though they are far ahead of me. Nobody knows what the future brings, so treat people with respect, as equals, and be friendly.

Although I have long since retired from teaching, I have not retired from life. I am not yet tired of doing little things for others and myself. It is my hope that anyone who reads this book would learn something from it. Don't be overwhelmed by the superfluity and cares of the world. It is a fleeting show, only heaven is perfectly true.

This book is my legacy to my children, family, community, country, and the world. I want to be remembered as a teacher, as someone who invested her life in helping others learn, giving them a solid foundation upon which to achieve their God-given goals.

What do you want to be known for?

*I want to be remembered as a teacher, as someone
who invested her life in helping others learn
and giving them a solid foundation
upon which to achieve their God-given goals.*

– Silverline Dennis Dic-Fiberesima

www.ingramcontent.com/pod-product-compliance
Lightning Source LLC
Chambersburg PA
CBHW050251120526
44590CB00016B/2304